Devotions from Moose Manor

A Tale of Forgiveness

Judi Collins

WESTBOW
PRESS®
A DIVISION OF THOMAS NELSON
& ZONDERVAN

All Scripture quotations in this publications are from The Message. Copyright © by Eugene H. Peterson 1993, 1994, 1995, 1996, 2000, 2001, 2002. Used by permission of NavPress Publishing Group.

Scripture taken from the Holy Bible, NEW INTERNATIONAL VERSION®. Copyright © 1973, 1978, 1984 by Biblica, Inc. All rights reserved worldwide. Used by permission. NEW INTERNATIONAL VERSION® and NIV® are registered trademarks of Biblica, Inc. Use of either trademark for the offering of goods or services requires the prior written consent of Biblica US, Inc.

Scripture quotations taken from the Holy Bible, New Living Translation, Copyright © 1996, 2004. Used by permission of Tyndale House Publishers, Inc., Wheaton, Illinois 60189. All rights reserved.

Scripture taken from the King James Version of the Bible.

Scripture quotations taken from the New American Standard Bible®, Copyright © 1960, 1962, 1963, 1968, 1971, 1972, 1973, 1975, 1977, 1995 by The Lockman Foundation. Used by permission. (www.Lockman.org)

WestBow Press books may be ordered through booksellers or by contacting:

WestBow Press
A Division of Thomas Nelson & Zondervan
1663 Liberty Drive
Bloomington, IN 47403
www.westbowpress.com
1 (866) 928-1240

ISBN: 978-1-5127-1855-3 (sc)
ISBN: 978-1-5127-1856-0 (hc)
ISBN: 978-1-5127-1854-6 (e)

Library of Congress Control Number: 2015918306

Print information available on the last page.

WestBow Press rev. date: 12/28/2015

For my children:

Kelly, Monika, Deanna, Shea, Christian, Cody,
and each precious grandchild they have given me.

People in your life will let you down. But God is
always faithful.

Jesus asked His Father to forgive us as we forgive
others. I have repeated those words of The Lord's
Prayer hundreds of times; yet it took Larry Krantz
to remind me of God's precept.

The three most life-changing words you can say
to someone who has hurt you are: "I forgive you".

"I love you" is good too. And those words I reserve
for you.

Special thanks go to my sisters, Lynn Barnett and Joan LeVert, my mom, Elaine (Kiddie) Kaphen, and my best bud Ruby Walker. They encourage me, inspire me and love me more than I deserve.

Thank you to the girls of the Moose Manor Bible Study, who have been my cheerleaders on this project.

Also to Lynda Furr, who labored over the editorial process.

And Carol and Greg Smith, for the gracious gift of allowing me to stay in Moose Manor until this book was complete.

I love you each.

Contents

Devotions from Moose Manor

Jesus said, "Here's what I want you to do: Find a quiet secluded place so you won't be tempted to role-play before God. Just be there as simply and honestly as you can manage. The focus will shift from you to God, as you begin to sense His grace." (Matthew 6:6 MSG)

I found this quiet, secluded place in *Moose Manor,* the cottage God lent me when everything else around me had crumbled. It's not about the manor; it's about the invitation. "'Behold' He says, 'I stand at the door and knock. If anyone hears my voice and opens the door I will come in'" (Revelation 3:20 KJV).

I heard the knock and answered.

Jesus Never Fails

Jesus never fails. I did. We had been living large for nearly thirty years, in debt up to our eyeballs, when the housing market crashed. And as went the economy, so went my husband's job. Crushed with depression, he moved to Hollywood to "reinvent his career." I was left with two college-aged sons, his eighty-nine-year-old mom, who had lived with us for seventeen years, a huge home, debt, and badly bruised self-esteem. Within four months, the bank foreclosed on our home. I sold what I could, shipped the rest to California, and helped my sons and mother-in-law find places to live.

I spent an inordinate amount of time trying to make sense of it all and the rest of my time trying to find a place I could afford to rent. One day, I pulled up to a wonderful little cottage with a "For Sale" sign in front. The owner gave me about two hundred fifty thousand reasons why I couldn't move in—but I gave him my phone number and asked him to call me if he ever decided to rent.

Several weeks later he called, and God gave me a place to live for another year. The moose head I had found in an antique store so many years before would hang above my mantle. I christened the cottage Moose Manor.

> He heals the heartbroken and bandages
> up their wounds. Psalm 147:3 MSG.

I am a testimony to His faithfulness.

Jesus never fails. Neither will you. When you belong to Him, it's never over!

Sixty-Minute Principle

God sees beyond
rejection,
selfishness,
poor choices,
uncertainty,
confusion,
and avarice.

God reverses
emptiness,
foreclosure,
identity theft,
dwindling finances,
limitations,
job loss,
bankruptcy,
embarrassment,
and migraines.

God promises to restore
what the "locust has eaten."
Joel 2:25

From low points, focus on Him,
and you will understand why
"the weaker (you) get,
the stronger (you) become"
(2 Corinthians 12:10 MSG).

There is no shortcut. Restoration is
never quick. You cannot get through
sixty minutes in less than an hour.
God restores one day at a time.

Raindrops

I was stuck in a storm—raindrops winning, one to nothing, with wind as their coach. Have you ever been slammed from every direction by gravity-defying drops? The creator of the storm can calm the storm, but He is more likely to let the storm rage and calm you.

You can blame whomever you choose for the storm, but remember: God is the orchestrator. His symphony of drops is never intended to inundate you but to saturate, refresh, restore, repair, and replenish. The one who caused the storm is not in control of the storm. God is always stronger than your adversary, and if He allows the storm, He always has a purpose and a plan for your greater good. You are never left alone.

The creator of the raindrops and storms is also the creator of the sun, which still shines just above the storm. The Father of Light shines even more brightly just above your circumstances. Almighty God pours out His abundant love on you, providing a Son that will never fade.

Jesus said, "Right now I am storm-tossed. And what am I going to say? 'Father, get me out of this'? No, this is why I came in the first place. I'll say, 'Father, put your glory on display'" (John 12:27–28 MSG).

Let Go

God will rescue you. "'If you'll hold on to me for dear life,' says God, 'I'll get you out of any trouble. I'll give you the best of care, if you'll only get to know and trust me'" (Psalm 91:14–18 MSG).

God wants fabulous things for you, but it's impossible to bless you when your arms are full of earthly treasures. You have to make room in your life and allow Him to fill the empty space. Trust Him completely. A *little* trust is *no trust at all*. Either God is completely faithful or He's not. Anything He has for you outshines anything you are gripping. Be patient. He's working.

Trust the one who beat the odds and won impossible battles. Put the thing you are clutching in His hands, and look for God's infusion of excitement and celebration into your daily drudgery. Get ready to jump from the bleachers onto the field and into the action!

Ask God to help you separate the essentials from the burdens. Remember: He's walked through furnaces, lions' dens, and prisons. And He still does! Drop your burdens, and walk with Him.

What Lies Beneath

> Consider it a sheer gift, friends *when* tests and
> challenges come at you from all sides. (James 1:2
> MSG emphasis added)

When a marriage dies, there is no memorial service. Everything just
gets split, tucked away, sold, or left behind. There is no grave to visit,
and even the good memories are painful.

When looking back is hurtful, when looking forward is scary, check
out *what lies beneath.*

> Jesus said "Anyone who listens to my teaching and
> follows it is wise, like a person who builds a house
> on solid rock." (Matthew 7:24 NLT)

Building your house on the Rock is good, but being attached to the
Rock is better. "Within Christ, suffering produces perseverance;
perseverance, character; and character, hope" (Romans 5:4–5 NIV).

"Within Christ" is a position you take on purpose and for a purpose.
Your life will not suddenly become easy. But you will look at the
trip differently. Potholes become pivotal points, rockslides become
warnings, and if the road gets washed out completely, you know He
has a better path for you to take. He provides opportunity!

Climb that mountain, slide down that hill, and walk through that
valley. But look deeply to make sure the solid Rock of Jesus Christ
is what you are fixed upon. He is *what lies beneath.*

Foreclosure

Tomorrow at 9:00 a.m., the bank will lock the house I have lived in for twenty-four years. Thanks to foreclosure, another one bites the dust. I visited the big house last night, and I had never felt so alone. The power had been turned off, and the darkness was suffocating. Armed with two flashlights and cuticle scissors (you know, to cut through the darkness and the bad guys), I plowed into the hollow, dead black space once filled with the laughter and light of a large family, and stuff—*lots of stuff*!

In the void, I scavenged through the remnants left behind to grab what I could before morning. I was out of time and money. Staying on task was difficult because I kept wading through memories of better days. Just as the situation became a bit too heavy, in walked my sister and my kids, throwing light beams from their headlamps and smiles. For the last time, we laughed our way through the darkness, making a few more memories in a house gone sad.

I drove away and didn't look back. The blessings I had been given would come with me, permanently, and the things I had given up were just temporary. "The Lord gives and the Lord takes away" (Job 1:21).

I carried away as much as my heart could hold and realized that because of the gift of life given to me by way of the manger so many years ago, I would spend eternity in His light, alongside my most precious possessions—the ones that matter most.

Nobody can foreclose on that!

Onward

Walking backward is never the way out of any difficult situation. Backward-walkers waste time blaming people. Christ walks forward. He's already replaced what you have lost—though you may not even see it yet. Never lose sight of what He is doing. You may already be on a new path. But keep focused upon your Leader. He will sensitize you to each new blessing. God offers new gifts and opportunities, showing you once again that out of the muddy waters of the Jordan River comes clarity. Don't resist the walk through the rushing river if that is the way He takes you. His path is always toward purification.

Given time, you will do it wrong again; but you can straighten things out in the control room, on your knees. And like Job, you can say, "I admit I once lived by rumors of You; now I have it all firsthand—from my own eyes and ears! I'm convinced: You can do anything and everything. Nothing and no one can upset Your plans" (Job 42:1 MSG)

The apostle Paul said a big amen to Job fifteen hundred years later when he wrote, "What is more, I consider everything a loss because of the surpassing worth of knowing Christ Jesus, my Lord, for whose sake I have lost all things. I consider them garbage, that I may gain Christ" (Philippians 3:8 MSG)

> You're off to great places, today is your day.
> Your mountain is waiting so get on your way.[1]

---

[1]   Dr. Seuss, *Oh, the Places You'll Go.* New York: Random House, 1990.

Joy!

Nine months of self-pity does not give birth to anything beautiful. But one month of praise does. Her name is *Joy,* and she has been born again into my life. For a while, I lost sight of her because I lost sight of my source. But my source never lost sight of me. I had so many questions. I still don't have the answers, but because I have given the whole mess up to God, I can see joy more clearly now.

He will quench the dry, parched patches of my life simply because I give Him time and opportunity. Purposely! Look for joy in the unpredictable events of the future, not because you're a visionary but because you trust the one who is. He says, "I will never, no never, no never leave you." And He means it. Neither you nor I will always walk in a state of exuberance or necessarily uprightness. But we will never be damaged beyond God's repair. The Doctor has always been in, and He gives something better than happiness. Her name is Joy.

> Work at getting along with each other and with God. Otherwise you'll never get so much as a glimpse of God. Make sure no one gets left out of God's generosity. Keep a sharp eye out for weeds of bitter discontent. A thistle or two gone to seed can ruin the whole garden in no time. (Hebrews 12:14–15 MSG)

Happiness depends upon happenings; Joy depends upon Jesus.

Knock-Knock

"Who's there?"

"It's me, Judi. Can I come in?"

"You can and you may."

There is a little smile in His voice. The door is massive, but it opens easily. The moment He sees me, He steps down from His throne and greets me with a hug. (When God hugs you, you know you've been hugged!)

"Come sit over here in the comfy seats," He says, "and tell me about that thing that is bothering you." (He's Red-Sea, walls-of-Jericho capable!)

Before I weigh my words, I spit out, "Bad headache." He doesn't roll His eyes, but I cringe at how petty it sounds.

Recognizing my embarrassment, He says, "My dear little Judi, nothing is too small. That thing bothering you bothers Me, because I love you so."

When you begin to realize the capacity of the love of God, you will position yourself for expectation! David knew it when he wrote, "But I will sing of your strength, in the morning I will sing of your love for you are my fortress, my refuge in times of trouble" (Psalm 59:16 NIV).

Go meet Him, and bring that thing that bothers you. Knock on His mighty door, and expect Him to answer. Always. You're in for a great visit!

"It's Not You. It's Him."

When somebody leaves you behind, loving family and friends all tell you, "It's not you; it's him."

But as far as you can tell, you're the one walking across the broken bridge. When you know God, you realize you are not alone. He is walking across that broken bridge with you. He has broken the laws of physics; weight is never an issue with God. His weight always supports your weight. Thank Him for every step you take. Thank Him for showing you how to step over the bad boards and for keeping you focused on the other side. Although you cannot see it, you know He does. He's already been there. God endures, abides, and repairs your bridge as you are walking. He makes sense of it all.

You may never get across the bridge if you focus upon the brokenness, upon statistics, upon the expectations of others. Don't spend a moment more looking back. Your shoulda-coulda-wouldas have kept you in the same place for too long. God never intended any one of us to live on the bridge but to walk across with Him.

Intentionally trust the one who restores brokenness better than ever.

It's not me; it's Him.

> He heals the brokenhearted and bandages up their wounds. (Psalm 147:3 MSG)

I Heart You

Unfailing love is
bigger than a heart,
but it is the same color.

Unfailing love is
spoken in action rather
than ecstasy, expectation,
or reward.

You can always count on
unfailing love to put your
best interest, peace, and joy
ahead of everything else.

There is no drama in
unfailing love.
It's a game of show,
not just tell.

Unfailing love is saturated
with a desire to be with you,
against all odds, allegiant,
faithful, honest, and open.

Unfailing love bled for you,
died for you,
lost His color so you
wouldn't lose yours.

> Trust in His *unfailing love* and rejoice in your
> salvation. (Psalm 13:5 NIV)

Lean

The free-standing bell tower in Pisa, Italy, had a bad start. By the time builders realized the foundation was poor, it was too late! "Let the thing settle for another hundred years," one of the builders suggested, and everyone thought it was a good idea. A century later, the new crew kicked up construction, adding more stories, seven bells, and a clock. But they never addressed the foundational issue. And of course the tower began to lean even more. Engineers came up with another not-so-brilliant quick fix: "Add more to one side!"[2] The builders aren't embarrassed anymore. They're dead.

If you are leaning, crumbling, or just unstable, check your foundation. God is capable of supporting and strengthening you at every stage of construction, no matter how you began or where you are planted. "The fundamental fact of existence is that this trust in God, this faith, is the firm foundation under everything that makes life worth living. It's our handle on what we can't see" (Hebrews 11:1–2 MSG).

"Trust in the Lord with all your heart and lean not on your own understanding," (Proverbs 3:5 KJV) or anyone else's! Never build ahead of God, who built you in the first place, who gave His life to erase your imperfection, and who is holding you up!

Trust Him—and lean like Pisa.

---

2   William Harris, "Will the Leaning Tower of Pisa ever fall?" March 16, 2011. HowStuffWorks.com. <http://science.howstuffworks.com/engineering/structural/will-leaning-tower-of-pisa-fall.htm> Accessed August 26, 2015.

Idols

I've let someone I love become an idol, and he's let me down. Is it his fault? Nope, it's mine. Idol worship has put us both into precarious positions. It is never anyone's job to live up to my expectations.

Admitting I'm guilty of idol worship is awkward. I was always so hard on those golden-calf guys who poured their affection into something powerless to deliver. "They followed worthless idols and themselves became worthless" (2 Kings 17:15 NIV).

Only God is in a position to be worshiped. If your life revolves around someone or something else, everyone will suffer. Idol worship is a real blessing-stopper. No person, thing, or achievement deserves a pedestal. No person or thing can deliver to your expectations except God alone. As Jonah said, "those who cling to worthless idols turn away from God's love for them" (Jonah 2:9 NIV).

The pedestal was your idea; God's idea for a perfect relationship centers around His Son, Jesus Christ. He left you His Spirit to walk with you and work with you every minute of every day.

> The Lord will keep you from all harm—He will watch over your life; the Lord will watch over your coming and going both now and forevermore. (Psalm 121:7–8 NIV)

"No other gods, only Me," God said.

Golden, chrome-plated, or flesh-toned!

Tag

Jump rope, hide-and-seek, and tag! These were the games of my youth unplugged. Ten of us squeezed Marco Polo into an eight-foot-wide blow-up pool. Tag was more user-friendly, but the game gave me the willies. I knew a simple tag didn't hurt, but the thought of being hunted down often left me crouched in the corner, squealing. Do you ever find yourself crouched in a corner, just waiting for someone to tag you? "You're it!" You don't know what—just *it*!

Fanny Crosby spent her life in darkness, but she never ran from anything. She had already been tagged by God for His purpose, and Fanny stood in the light, totally covered by the shadow of the Almighty.

From inside her blindness, Fanny wrote these words:

> He hideth my soul in the cleft of the rock
> That covers the dry, thirsty land;
> He hideth my life in the depths of His love
> And covers me there with His hand
>
> —"He Hideth My Soul,"
> Fanny J. Crosby, 1890

When you don't have the strength to fight, and crouching feels more natural, reach out and grab God's strength.

Know who needs Him most?

Tag. You're it.

Open Hands

I'm a clencher. If anyone points it out, I do the hand stretch, my physical version of denial. But morning fingernail marks in my palms are strong indicators: sometime in the night, I clenched!

It's hard to let go, especially when it's been your life's job to protect, preserve, defend, shield, insulate, and shelter. Then one day everybody flies away, and you are left with nothing to clench. Clenched handfuls of emptiness are breeding grounds for bitterness, hopelessness, and self-pity. If you are clenching, *it's time to let go.* God always replaces your idea of good for His idea of better—His strength for your weakness, His abundance for your emptiness, a new direction out of your dead end.

Trust in the Lord to work in your circumstance. It's not over. This is not your last anything. God restores. Always. He will fill your hands once again, providing and blessing you in response to your trust.

> Get rid of all bitterness, rage, anger, harsh words and slander, as well as all types of evil behavior. (Ephesians 4:31 NLT)

God fills open hands, but He won't pry open your clenchers just to squeeze stuff in. Flatten out your grabbers, stretch those fingers to heaven, and expect Him to fill you with "good and perfect gifts."

Ten to *one*, He does it!

Monkey Bars

Getting over a painful experience is much like crossing monkey bars. You have to let go at some point in order to move forward.

—C. S. Lewis

"Hang in there! Don't let go!" Friends rave on, not knowing how tired you are. You lunge to your next bar, and somebody shouts, "You're halfway there!" You are exhausted, but when you look down, you realize the drop may be more painful than pushing your way across. So you grab the next rung. Now they are chanting your name phonetically.

Above the drumbeat of the cheering and confusion, you hear a still, small voice: "*Trust Me*," God reminds you. Your hope should be built on nothing less.

When you are just hanging there, let Him work in your life. But don't be content just hanging in. *Hang in Christ*, who gives you enough strength for that bar, for that moment, and for the next. One rung at a time.

> So keep a firm *grip* on the faith. The suffering won't last forever. It won't be long before this generous God who has great plans for us in Christ—eternal and glorious plans they are—will have you put together and on your feet for good. (1 Peter 5:9 MSG)

Fill 'Er Up

"Are you tired of life's repetition? Worn out? Burned out on religion? Come to Me. Get away with Me and you'll recover your life. I'll show you how to take a real test. Walk with Me and work with Me—watch how I do it. Learn the unforced rhythms of grace. I won't lay anything heavy or ill fitting on you. Keep company with Me and you'll learn to live freely and lightly" (said Jesus). (Matthew 11:28–30 MSG)

You cannot run on empty for long. When stopping at the pump seems like a waste of time, remember: what you gather at the pump will enable you to go the distance. Give yourself some time at the pump. Take God at His Word. Then respond: "Fill 'er up!"

Fill 'er up comes during moments of stillness with your eyes on the one who can get stuff done. He works inside/out and has in view a much greater victory than the one you imagine. Take the minutes you need to be refreshed and filled. Slow down to a halt. Read the Bible. Pray. Praise Him. You may decide to stick around longer in this haven of restoration.

God said: "I'll refresh tired bodies; I'll restore tired souls." (Jeremiah 31:25 MSG)

To which you should reply, "Fill 'er up."

Zero Dark Thirty

It's four thirty in the morning. Can't sleep. Nothing outside my house seems to be having any trouble. Moonlight splashes through the bare trees onto my yard. It's peaceful out there. Nature is once again ignoring my internal frenzy. I know detox is always provided during quiet time with God, reading the worlds spoken by His Son, and praying. But I don't want to get out of bed; I want to sleep.

Never waste the wake-up call. When God wakes you up, He isn't prompting you to hash over those things that bothered you yesterday or instigating worry about what tomorrow may bring. Talk to Him. Listen to Him. He promises another day in His unfailing love, where God provides a glorious do-over.

> I pray to the Lord, and He answers me. He frees me
> from all my fears. Because I look to Him for help,
> He gives me His radiance of joy. He hears the ache
> in my soul. He heals me. (Psalm 34:4–6)

His promises still stand strong.

> The light shines in the darkness, and the darkness
> can never extinguish it. (John 1:5 NLT)

Sun's coming up.

Roads

> Whether you turn to the right or to the left, your
> ears will hear a voice behind you, saying: "This is
> the way; walk in It." (Isaiah 30:21 NIV)

Are you standing at the place where the road ends and forest begins?
Lucky for you—I just saw God standing right there. He's pointing
to the woods, saying, "Don't be afraid; follow Me. I've done this
before."

"This is the way; walk in it."

He heads in first. Follow Him. Or not. You've got other choices.
Interstate highways will take you where you are going faster, and the
ride will be smoother than the trek through the woods. But if you
stick to the main highways, you may never experience the victories
God unravels in the untraveled places. You cannot walk too far
from the love of God, which is in Christ Jesus. God has made you
the beneficiary of His companionship. His care is predictable. He
has a proven track record. But don't just stand there expecting to be
teleported. It is up to you to take steps.

> And God said to Abraham, walk through the
> country, its length and breadth; I'm giving it all to
> you. (Genesis 13:15 MSG)

> Jesus said, "I am the road, the truth and the life.
> No one gets to the Father apart from me." (John
> 14:6 MSG)

Peace

> And the peace of God, which surpasses all
> understanding, will guard your hearts and minds
> through Christ Jesus. (Philippians 4:7 NKJV)

"Peace that passes understanding" are encouraging words during
funerals, failures, and fractures. But God offers us more: His peace
surpasses understanding. That is passing with muscle!

> Be anxious for nothing, but in everything by prayer
> and supplication, with thanksgiving, let your
> requests be made known to God. (Philippians 4:6)

God always goes way above and beyond what we expect. The dead
ends of our lives are never dead ends to God. If today is muddled
with confusion and clutter, aimlessness, loss of hope, and happiness,
grab this verse:

> Be anxious for nothing, but in everything, by
> prayer and supplication, with thanksgiving, let your
> requests be made known to God. And the peace
> that *surpasses* all understanding, will guard your
> hearts and minds through Christ Jesus.

Directions: Take this verse every hour or as needed. You cannot
overdose, and the side effects are awesome.

Ache

Inspirational words for my morning blog often come in the middle of the night. If I don't immediately write them down, by morning they're gone. In the middle of last night, I got an idea. Too lazy to walk to the kitchen for my laptop, I blindly patted the bedside table for a pen and paper. I landed a Sharpie, and went paperless writing this one-word reminder on my palm: ACHE.

Sharpies brag permanent ink. By the world's standards that means at least three days. The word would remain etched into my palm long after the hurt had dissipated.

God's perfect solution often takes you on a walk of inconvenience. But during that walk, He delivers you from what seems like indelible pain and shows you that in Him, pain is never permanent. When the ache comes into your life, step out of your comfort zone and into His.

> So we fix our eyes not on what is seen, but on what is unseen, since what is seen is temporary, but what is unseen is eternal. (2 Corinthians 4:18 KJV)

The Good Shepherd carries a rod for defense and a staff to lead. But I find no mention of a permanent marker to chart our feelings or hurts. Maybe that's because in Christ, *the ache is never permanent.*

> I'll convert their weeping into laughter lavishing comfort, invading their grief with joy. (Jeremiah 31:13 MSG)

Joy! Write *that* on your hand with a Sharpie!

Alone.

Alone is just a feeling, not a place. When you know Christ, "alone" is out of the question. *Alone is where God works miracles.*

John the Baptist prophesied alone.

John the beloved wandered the isle of Patmos and wrote the book of Revelation alone.

Alone was where

- David fought lions and giants;
- Joseph was sold into slavery;
- Paul wrote one-third of the New Testament; and
- Jesus died in our place.

Alone is where you cling to the one who makes it impossible to be alone. When you experience the feeling of overwhelming loneliness, you have the perfect setup for time with your Creator. Crack open your Bible. (John is a great place to start.) Pray as you go, and praise Him for sharing these words and this Savior with you. He's beside you right now, the "I-will-never-leave-you-nor-forsake-you."

> He meant what He said,
> And said what He meant
> Your Father is faithful
> One hundred percent![3]
> (My apologies to Dr. Seuss)

---

[3] Philip Nel, *Dr. Seuss: American Icon*. (New York: Continuum International Publishing Company, 2004) 113.

Best Years

"She gave him the best years of her life," somebody said. Don't you wonder which ones they were? And if she gave them away, are there none left?

Which years do you consider to be your best? Did you give them away? Do you want them back? What will you do with them when you get them? Your life was designed to bless another life, so those years were not lost. You were being polished!

If you gave away your "best years," it doesn't mean you're done. God's supply room is still full. And giving gifts is one of His favorite things.

If, by chance, you still believe you have lost or given away your best years, I hope you have at least seeded a blessing in someone's life. God loves a cheerful giver.

And He will bless you beyond the gift.

> Give and it will be given to you. A good measure,
> pressed down, shaken together and running over.
> (Luke 6:38 MSG)

Attachment

I am the vine; you are the branches. If you remain
in me and I in you, you will bear much fruit; apart
from me, you can do nothing. (John 15:5 NIV)

Have you ever been pruned back just about the time you were about
to bud? Remember: your hopes for a plentiful harvest can never be
dashed when you are attached to the True Vine.

God promises life on His Vine is productive. His promise is not "if
you remain in me, you may be able to produce much fruit." He has
committed His full promise to you: "You will produce much fruit,
if you remain in Me and I in you."

He actively participates in your life—in your growth and
productivity—when you stay attached. He may cut away the weeds
that grow around you before they pull you away. The result? You'll
have more room to grip!

Attach yourself to Christ. You will prosper in the connection. "When
you're joined with Me and I in you, the relation intimate and organic,
the harvest is sure to be abundant. Separated, you can't produce a
thing" (John 15:6–8 MSG).

But attached? Bumper crop!

Because You Ask

At the call of God's name, He's there, which is why He gets so troubled when you use His name unnecessarily. God has the power to pull you out of the ditch immediately, but more often, because He loves you and wants to teach you powerful lessons, He alters slowly. Never rush Him. Always defer to His timetable, not yours, and be willing to bend. If you won't, He may go somewhere else for your blessing.

From nothing comes something. He's really good at that. Bit by bit, your burden becomes lighter *because you ask.*

He works in the garden of your life, and you prosper *because you ask.*

He's moving mountains and killing fleas, changing hearts and minds, and making fuzzy things clear *because you ask.*

If you're feeling slighted, remember: "You have not because you ask not" (James 4:3 KJV).

Progressively, He reveals. Positively, He improves *because you ask.*

The Change

I'm standing at the corner of Muddled and Needy, waiting for the bus to take me somewhere to do something. The job market isn't flowing with opportunity for: older woman with typing skills; a cracker-jack at shorthand, who speaks a few words of Norwegian and Russian and makes a mean pot of coffee.

The change of life came late for me, and I was thrown into the wind, expected to fly—with arthritic wings! I never understood the aeronautical principle, but my best friend runs the control tower. He says I can fly, and I have no reason to doubt Him. He's never steered me wrong. There has been a change in my situation, and I'm looking for a job. My limitations are of no consequence to God, who sees my potential differently. He is orchestrating the change.

Instead of tooting my own horn on LinkedIn, I should post this testimony:

> Older woman seeks to thank the one who puts her in the right place at the right time. She is a grateful recipient of good gifts and a believer in daily bread. While she walks through the shadow of lean times, she knows even in the fruitful days, she was never her own provider. And even if she had been, she never could have provided as well as the one who allowed her to go through *the change.*

Question

Does the Lord love me more when I am fasting and praying or when I am working hard? Does He love me more when I struggle to find time to spend with Him or when I get ahead of His plan?

When I teach or when I learn?

When I'm fearful or when I'm confident?

When I trust Him to pull me out or when I try to do it myself?

When I am surrounded or when I am alone?

The answer is, of course, "Yes. He does."

Are you living on purpose? Take another look. If you are trying to manipulate perfection, or at least the perception of perfection, you're missing the mark. Perfection is held in the hands of the Creator, who "keeps you in perfect peace when you keep your eyes on Him." (Isaiah 26:3) His power is shown through your weakness, every hour, every day, moment by moment, mistake after mistake. His power is yours for the asking.

Does God love you more when you succeed or when you fail? When you're on your knees praying your heart out or when you are talking to Him behind the steering wheel of your car? The answer is always *yes*.

Any questions?

Bless Them

> Bless those who curse you pray for those who mistreat you. (Luke 6:28 NIV)

Now, let me get this right: I'm supposed to ask God to bestow divine favor on the one causing my angst. I'm seriously not feeling it, so I try wording it differently:

> Lord, You know that person who tore me apart and ripped my heart out? Bless them. (Sounds like I should have added "in the gut or in the butt.")

I start over.

> What I mean to ask You, Lord, is that You give them Your divine favor (after You've slapped them around a bit).

Clearing my throat, I clarify.

> By "favor" I mean bring them into Your fold. By "fold" I mean surround them with those who love You, and by "those who love You," I mean "those who are willing to mold to Your likeness." By "likeness" I mean Your perfection. *You*, who despises sin, love us beyond all measure.

And suddenly it all becomes clear:

> Father, bring that person back to the fullness of Your creation, not to the expectations of mine. Restore them to the greatness that You intended for them all along. Give them *Your* special favor. Out of my hands, Lord, into Yours. Bless them!

And finally, I get it.

Jesus Lives in a Little House

His yard is filled with pines, a few hardwoods, birds, and squirrels. If you're not paying attention to the Way, you can get lost in dozens of distractions.

You're never too far from Jesus's little house, wherever you live. *It's an on-purpose route to an unbroken place.*

Pack light! You won't really need anything but a good appetite and genuine faith. Inside Jesus's house, your burden may seem less important. But share your troubles with Him anyway. He's big on reflection and release.

Do you know the way to His house? It's easy to find—easier, in fact, than clicking your heels together three times and saying, "There's no place like home." Jesus told us how to get there over two thousand years ago, and God hasn't moved. "Seek first the kingdom of God, and His righteousness, and all these things shall be added unto you" (Matthew 6:33 NKJV).

You will never fully recognize the things He can do in your life until you completely trust Him. Spend time in His presence and you will begin to identify His presents. He works things in your life together for His greater purpose.

Jesus lives in a little house. Make sure it's yours.

Casting

Humble yourselves under the mighty hand of God,
that He may exalt you in due time; Casting all
your cares upon Him, for He cares for you. (1 Peter
5:6–7 KJV)

In the mighty hand of God, you are protected from evil. He will lift
you up in *due time*. A relationship with Him is a daily deal: unless
you keep casting, you will never receive the full benefit of the catch.

My son Cody loves fly-fishing. He dances the line in the air, then
tosses it into the deeper water where the really good fish live. But the
line doesn't lay there. Cody slowly drags it over to the shore, where
the casting process begins all over again.

Imagine yourself in the mighty hand of God. You must realize by now
He's the better part of your team. Casting is active and interactive.
All good relationships must be. Give God your tangled line, and
trust Him when He untwists the knots and throws you into the
deep. Humble yourself before Him. When things go wrong, when
you're bobbing up and down in the water with no clear direction,
ask yourself, _Who's the better fisherman in this scenario?_

He will restore, support and strengthen you, and
He will place you on a firm foundation. (1 Peter
5:10 NLT)

Elephant

"Eat an elephant one bite at a time," my sister Joan reminds me when I am completely overwhelmed. She says, "Problems are like elephants. They're born big and eat a lot, and the longer they sit on you, the harder they crush."

When problems come to you in herds—and they usually do—separate the pack. If you look at your problems all at once, you're in for a pachydermic nightmare.

Dr. Paul Walker, Mt. Paran Church of God, says, "Your problem is not the problem. Your problem is your approach to the problem, and that is not a problem, it's an opportunity!" Open your Bible, and take a look at some of those who took their opportunities to God. He has a list of fabulous solutions!

You may never part the waters of the Chattahoochee River or notice frogs overtaking your enemy's house, but you know absolutely, "God works all things together for good, for them that love Him and are called according to His purpose." (Romans 8:28) Make sure you are in that group. It's a matter of acuity. Keep your senses sharpened to every victory God gives you. You can trust Him in all things.

Jesus said, "Come unto Me all you who are weary and carry heavy burdens, and I will give you rest" (Matthew 11:28 NLT).

Give Him back the elephant.

Stakkels Mig

My great-aunts (old Danish women) would remain seated around the Sunday dinner table long after dessert, and discuss things Scandinavian. From the size of their diamonds to the men in their lives to ill-fitting bras, this group complained with flair! When the griping reached the pinnacle of Danish exasperation, one old aunt would invariably place the back of her hand to her forehead, tip her chin toward heaven, and moan, "*Stakkels mig*" (pronounced "staggles my"). And all the other aunts would translate in sing-songy English, "Poor me."

When Jesus came out of the desert, He joined the disciples without a complaint (Luke 4). He had every right to "stakkels mig," but He knew complaining to them would be of no benefit. Because the only one who could help Him was His Father. Jesus was a child of the King. And so are you! "Pile your troubles on God's shoulders. He will carry your load He will help you out" (Psalm 55:22 MSG).

God welcomes complaints. "Stakkels mig" your heart out to the only one who can turn exasperations inside/out. *Jesus hashed things over with His Dad, and so should you.*

Complain with flair

- like David the shepherd boy did.
- like Abraham, the father of the Hebrew nation.
- like Jonah and Jeremiah and Isaiah did.

Get real with your griping! Regardless of your nationality, God understands and is fully capable of providing just what you need!

The Good Stuff

My mom and dad introduced me to Jesus Christ, by example of their love for Him, each other, and me. They left me with their most valuable possessions—their advice:

1. Jesus plus nothing equals everything.
2. Scandinavian blood running through my veins is a perk.
3. Cleanliness is next to godliness.
4. Underwear should never be ripped.
5. Whiskey ruins people.
6. Baptists will be first into heaven.

Good stuff! But my parents actually gave me everything I needed at number 1, when they led me to Christ. Good underwear, strong bloodlines, and germ-killing products don't fully resolve any issues. And I'm certain Baptists are going to have to stand in line with the wicked whiskey-drinkers who have accepted Christ.

Regardless of your heritage, Christ has given you a new identity through His bloodline. He restores inside-out!

Your torn secrets may be displayed in awkward circumstances, but He will clothe you with the newness of His being. "If anyone is in Christ he is a new creature; the old things are passed away; behold all things are become new" (2 Corinthians 5:17 KJV).

Horns

Blessed are those who fear the Lord, who find great delight in His commands. They will have no fear of bad news; their hearts are steadfast trusting in the Lord. Their hearts are secure, they will have no fear in the end and will look in triumph on their foes. They have freely scattered their gifts to the poor, their righteousness endures forever, their 'horn' will be lifted high in honor. (Portions of Psalm 112 NIV)

This acrostic poem begins "Praise God," which is practically impossible to do when you're loaded down with problems. Take a minute and warm up to the idea: praise God. Focus on who He is and what He does, "and good will come. No fear of bad news, steadfast hearts, security, triumph … and horns. I could have done without the horns—but that must come with the Psalm 112 package.

The biblical application of the word *horn* translates to "dignity." My Scandinavian ancestors must have missed the visual picture of dignity, because nothing says "Norwegian woman" like a chunky broad in a metal bra and horned hat, singing arias of warning as she readies herself to charge the enemy. I choose not to look like but to be that girl.

Claim God's promise for security, triumph, no fear of bad news, a steadfast heart … *and horns.*

Sa Fars Sa Gud

Oliver Gustav Thorpe (1888–1979) was "Unkie" to me.

My great uncle immigrated to America from Norway when he was only sixteen. As far as I remember, he always wore a suit, tie, hat, and overcoat and galoshes when necessary. Each day he walked from his one-room apartment to the same small Chicago diner for his meals. He dined alone.

Every other Friday, Unkie filled his shopping bag with Pepsi and Fannie Mae Candy and took the train west from Chicago, to our home in Villa Park, Illinois. During those visits, he shared his observations:

- "Vitout potatoes, it's not really dinner."
- "Dat man who died on my story (soap opera) isn't really dead. I yust saw him on annuder show last night."
- "God puts money on da sidevaks, so when you valk, alvays look down."

But the most important thing Unkie shared with us was his unwavering faith in Jesus. No matter when you asked Unkie, "How's it going?" his reply was always, "Sa far sa gud." No matter how you say it in English, "so far so good" should be your response too.

> For I have chosen you and will not throw you away. Don't be afraid for I am with you. Don't be discouraged for I am your God. I will strengthen you and help you. I will hold you up with my victorious right hand. (Isaiah 41:9–10 NLT)

Once you are vested in Christ, no matter where you are or who are with (or without), you can always say, "Sa far sa gud."

Locusts

It was 1958. Villa Park, Illinois. I was awakened by an eerie whining sound. The crescendo sent me running downstairs to consult my resource, "Momma-pedia." She had answers! "Seventeen-year locusts," she said. "Won't hurt you, they're just loud."

For the next two months, we lived among the swarming Cicadas, vegetarians thankfully, who ate their way through the summer. ("One locust can eat its weight in plants every day. A swarm of locusts can eat up to four hundred million pounds of plants each day!" (Easyscienceforkids.com/all-about-locusts)

As quickly as they came, they went—leaving yards and trees filled with their sticky, empty carcasses. I was glad they were dead. Thing is, they weren't. They had simply hatched, rebooted, and returned underground to live another seventeen years or so. The destruction that summer was horrific. Crops and landscapes were ruined. *But God restores ruined things.*

When you trust God in everything, He works in your life.

Joel 2:25 is just another one of His promises: "I will repay you for the years the locusts have eaten" (NIV).

The Crusts

When Mamaw turned eighty-nine, I threw a tea party in her honor.
I dug out the old fancy recipes Mamaw enjoyed as a young woman.
She could never fully appreciate the skimpy salads the size-four ladies
eat for lunch these days. In the 1930s tuna noodle casserole was a
food group.

Digging out the old recipes, I found the favored four-layer sandwich
loaf/cake, stuffed with three different yet equally rich fillings and
frosted with cream cheese. I knew the older ladies at this party would
be dazzled.

I was wrong: Mamaw couldn't see what she was eating and became
confused. My mom saw it but didn't recognize it, defending herself
by telling me, "It's probably because you forgot to cut the crusts off
the loaf, which makes the frosting lumpy." (Lumpy is never good.)

Twenty-five hundred years ago, Isaiah saw the importance of
"smooth": "Make the road straight and smooth a highway fit for
our God. Fill in the valleys, level off the hills, smooth out the ruts,
clear out the rocks" (Isaiah 40:3–5 MSG).

What lumps are separating you from perfection? Ask God to scrape
them off. The process is uncomfortable but necessary, especially if
you are asking Him for frosting. When your crusts are gone, trust
Him to perfect your presentation, and the glory of the Lord, and
the loaf, will follow.

Next year's tea party, these little old ladies are getting a can of Boost.

Pepperlily

I was in the doctor's office with the flu the day Kelly called to ask, "Where *are* you, Mom, and who is at home with Mamaw? Pepperlily died!" Kelly sobbed.

Pepperlily had been part of our family for more than twenty years. Our deaf and blind Jack Russell Terrier had lately become the perfect pet for my eighty-nine-year-old mother-in-law, who shared the same disabilities.

Ashamed to admit it, I had dreamed of the day when this agonizing barker and random tinkler would meet her maker. But when I heard Pepperlily had died, I began to cry. Mamaw had lost another companion. Kelly continued her phone call: "I told Mamaw I would leave work and be right there. But Mom, when I asked Mamaw where Pepperlily was at the moment, she answered, 'I reckon she's in a bettah place.'"

Kelly and I both began laughing hysterically through our tears. Kelly and our friend Nela rushed home from the office to find Pepperlily laying in her elaborate doggy bed, *still* for the first time in her life. In reverence, Kelly bent to kiss Pepperlily's cheek, when up popped Pepperlily!

Kelly screamed, "She's alive!"

I've been laughing all day, which has taken the focus off my own flulike symptoms. God gives us the ridiculous things in life so we can learn to laugh.

So laugh—hard and often! Pepperlily may not be in a "bettah place," but I am!

The Wow Factor

G. K. Chesterton said, "There are two ways to get enough; one is to accumulate more and more. The other is to desire less."[4]

God took me from living not-so-simply back to simple where I belong. My faith is simple; I believe God sent His only Son, Jesus Christ, for me. I didn't qualify for this gift. I just accepted it. "Thank You so much" is an inadequate response, but it's all I've got. I'm counting on John 3:16, "For God so loved ... He sent." I am the "whosoever" in that verse. Does that make me special? I'd like to think so, but no. He offers you the same gift.

I have done nothing to qualify for such an extravagant amount of love except to bring my dirty laundry to Him and ask Him to clean me up. Concerned I might miss something, I bring it all—the dingy, soiled, and almost clean—and let Him sort it all out. He said He would, and He did, and He does, and He will. Who wouldn't want to be attached to that kind of perfection!

"Close to Him" is where I gauge my performance. Close is where I find His joys—"New every morning" (Lamentations 3:22).

Nobody is clamoring for my autograph or my time. Nobody is talking about my fabulous ministry or offering me a gig for a Bible rewrite. My life is simply "a wow" because my Savior is "a *wow*."

He loves me just the way I am, and He loves me too much to let me stay that way. Stand in the light of His *wow*!

---

4   www.chesterton.org/who-is-this-guy/

Five-in-One

Can't teach an old dog new tricks? Young or old, you'd better be learning, or you'll be left in dial-up mode. This past week, I painted my house and in the process learned

- how to pour paint into a tray;
- why you don't roll paint close to trim; and
- the value of tools like the five-in-one.

Isaiah advertised Jesus seven hundred years before He appeared. "Wonderful, Counselor, the Mighty God, the Everlasting Father, the Prince of Peace." And frankly, those names just touch the surface.

He is my go-to guy for everything. In hurt, sickness, loss, debt, pain, and rejection, I reach out. Jesus promises; Jesus serves. He leads me out of impossible situations. He sees the future, and if I hold Him close, He shows me what to do next. He is abundantly able to open, close, cut and seal, scrape, and smooth out the imperfections of life.

He makes me laugh at myself when I attempt to handle things on my own. When I revert back to my own hands, my "ten-in-two" will mess it up every time!

Eighty-Six It!

Chumley's Bar, New York, 1922: The Prohibition-era bar, equipped with trap doors and escape routes, had two entrances. Just before police raids, cops would phone the bar to warn the owner: "Eighty-six your customers." While everyone ran out the 86 Bedford Street exit, police entered the Barrow Street door.[5]

New York, 1947: Ten-table diner, forty-five people, one waitress scrambling between customers and one short-order cook. "Eighty-six the cherry pie, Marv," she squawks at the cook, giving the lady at table nine the evil eye.

Hollywood film set, 2005: The director pitches a hissy-fit and screams at the crew, "Somebody eighty-six the ugly sofa!"

What you would eighty-six if you could? Whatever is dragging you down—*eighty-six it* the Romans 8:6 way:

> Those who think they can do it on their own end up obsessed with measure their own moral muscle, but never get around to exercising it in real life. Those who trust God's action in them find that God's Spirit is in them—living and breathing God!" (Romans 8:6 MSG)

Is there something standing in the way of the joy God has promised you? *Eighty-six it!* Rethink the cherry pie.

---

[5]   Chumley's, www.wikipedia.org

Gifts

Christmas brings joy and hope, but too soon the glitter falls off the tree and winter's mood sinks back in. The hours beyond the manger require quiet reflection; Jesus is still Lord. He came for us. He lived in poverty so we could spend eternity in wealth. Your hope lies beyond the state of the union, the economy, personal limitations, or karma. Your hope is in the one who said:

> For truly I say to you, if you have the faith the size of a mustard seed, you will say to this mountain; "move from here to there" and it will move; and nothing will be impossible for you. (Matthew 17:20)

He moves mountains! He's done it for others—He's done it for me. You and I carry each other through prayer, but personal pain takes no passengers. Even the ones who tell you they "know how you feel" rarely do, but you love them for trying.

God has blessed me with the best friends, who have loved me through my worst and more often because of it. As I walk into the darkness of a new year, He lights my path, just enough for each step. And no gift I have gotten or given can touch the one God gives: eternal life through Jesus Christ. Starting now ... and the *gift* just keeps on giving.

All about Me

The stars of the Golden Globes, pinched and pulled together to outdazzle each other, appeared confident.

They had each lived for the moment that made *life all about them,* and as each one rose to accept their award, it was obvious: they were each their own favorite.

How many stars left their homes yesterday aware that Jesus was with them and would be throughout the evening award's show? How many of them would take advantage of the personal relationship He offers the winners and the losers? Did anybody recognize that God made it "all about them" two thousand years ago, when He sent His Son to earth to die in their place? Did they understand, His gift *is* the top award?

Last night's winners have one more trophy and fifteen more minutes of fame. The losers will find a way to appear nonchalant about the defeat, and Jesus will once again return to His throne, waiting for each of us, the winners and the losers, to knock on His door.

He listens, encourages, and comforts us, in love and understanding. Look beyond yourself to Jesus, the only *one* who has accurately shown "It's all about you."

> People look at the outward appearance; but the
> Lord looks at the heart. (1 Samuel 16:7 NIV)

Fizzing

Baking powder, a dry chemical leavening agent, is basically a gas bag. It is inert until it's mixed with other ingredients. Used in the proper way, baking powder does wonders; but in hot water on its own, it fizzes out of control.

As Christ said to Martha, "You're fussing far too much getting yourself worked up over nothing. One thing only is essential and Mary (your sister) has chosen it" (Luke 10:41–42 MSG).

Martha fizzed when she should have been content sitting at the feet of Jesus. God still holds your warranty and won't divulge your expiration date, which doesn't matter anyway, because in Him, you never expire. He is the one who gives you essence and recognizes your talent. He pulls you back in, to warn you against the consequences of fizzing beyond purpose.

I want my life to matter—to live beyond the can, to be mixed in with those I love, if only to make their loads lighter. And one day, He will turn to me and say, "Way to rise!"

There You Are!

My "bonus" daughter, DeAnna, never fusses because I am late returning a call. She responds to my tardiness with a smile in her voice: "There you are!" she greets. What a gift. "A friend loves at all times" (Proverbs 17:17 NKJV).

There have been days when I didn't place or return calls from God. But when my discipleship barometer registers low, what usually follows is an ache in my gut only His touch will heal. Slipping past the forgive-me-for-not-getting-back-to-you-sooner part, I head straight for the relationship. God knows I'm not the best friend. But He is, and though I cannot hear Him, I know He is saying, "There you are!" He never lost sight of me for a minute!

"I never lose sight of your love, but keep in step with you, never missing a beat," David wrote in Psalm 26:3 (MSG).

God accepts my leftovers and second-bests, although I am always His first choice. So are you! If you feel the need to play catch-up, indulge. But don't let it eat up precious time connecting to His Spirit. God is the perfect friend, who will always respond with a smile in His voice: "There you are!"

Hokey Pokey

When Jesus came to seek and save, He broke down the rules and the rulers of the game, with one word: *repent.* It wasn't a hokey pokey or a hocus pocus—it was a chance for a fresh start. Not everyone wanted to play His way. *It couldn't be that simple,* they thought.

Only a few had actually seen the horror of the sacrifice Christ gave to make it *simple* for us. Jesus gave Himself to exchange the emptiness of religion for the fullness of relationship. God offers His Son once, for all. *You can't win this game playing by your rules. His gift is based upon His love, not your game-playing abilities.*

> Walk with Me and work with Me—watch how I do it. Learn the unforced rhythms of grace. I won't lay anything heavy or ill fitting on you. Keep company with me and you'll learn to live freely and lightly. (Matthew 11:28 MSG)

Jesus loves you so much. But go ahead, if you must: "Put your right foot in, put your right foot out, put your right foot in, and then you shake it all about, you do the hokey pokey and your turn yourself around," and thank God, that's *not* what it all about!

Copying Copies

Are you an original or a copy? Idols are not born; they are manufactured, and copying them will change you into a watered-down version of a manufactured product. God never intended you to be a copy. You are His original!

Christ gave His life for the *original you*—the good, the bad, and the ugly you. He has a plan for your life, but you have to trust Him. On purpose! He will put you on higher ground.

Collectively we praise. Specifically we serve. If you are trying to be like someone else, you are diminishing your contribution. Copy Jesus, the original. Take the walk with Him. He never intended to remain on a pedestal, and neither should you.

> As obedient children, let yourselves be pulled into a
> way of life shared by God's life, a life energetic and
> blazing with holiness. God said, "I am holy; you be
> holy." (1 Peter 1:16 MSG)

Comparisons

When you compare yourself to others, you always compare your worst fault with their best feature.

God is the standard. He sees you in truth, while your perspective is limited and myopic. Feature-by-feature, God created you. Perfectly! In His image! You are a direct knock off! There is always room for improvement, but quality should be measured against His perfection, not some airbrushed, overexercised, undernourished image on the front of a magazine.

Physical beauty fades; God sees deeply into the "unfading beauty of a gentle and quiet spirit" (1 Peter 3:4 NLT).

You are here for a purpose. Stand up. Walk out of your way and smile at someone. Big smile. And thank God for your ability to bring joy to others who may be going through something horrible: *they may be comparing themselves to you!*

> Oh, yes You shaped me first inside, then out; You formed me in my mother's womb. I thank You, High God—You are breathtaking! Body and soul, I am marvelously made. (Psalm 139:14 MSG)

The Source

Somewhere, there's a power outage.
Somebody's sick.
Somebody's broke.
Somebody's confused.
Somebody's lost hope.
Somebody is looking for answers.
I am not their source. Neither are you.

God gave His perfect child to ease pain, erase worry, and wipe out fear. Jesus, the flawless Son of God, was given to us in exchange for our bad decisions. All we have to do to take advantage of this lopsided trade is accept the gift, give up control, and plug into the true power source. Lay down your quick fixes, and hit your knees. God is still in control.

> We take our lead from Christ who is the source of everything we do. He keeps us in step with each other. His very breath and blood flow through us, nourishing us so that we will grow up healthy in God, robust in love. (Ephesians 4:15 MSG)

But God is the never-ending power source. If you have already plugged in, you have seen what He can do. Now take the refresher course: remember what He has done, and acknowledge the promises of what He will do for the ones He loves.

> God's way is not a matter of mere talk; it's an empowered life. (1 Corinthians 4:20 MSG)

Dangling

God sees way down your road and isn't going to give you something today just to make you sick tomorrow. The God of comfort is not a dangler.

God is the "giver of good and perfect gifts" (James 1:17). His reputation is solid, and His timing is impeccable. If your life is full of the wrong things, where are you going to put the right things when they come your way? Never fear emptiness when you know God, who always has plans for that space. Trust God. You cannot "trust God, but …," because the word *but* deflates the balloon of trust.

He craves a relationship with you. Your life may not be working together as you dreamed, but when you depend upon Him, you know He is still working it out. And He works things out perfectly. If you don't get what you are asking for today, spend more time seeking His will for your life. Keep trusting. Don't be so rigid that you reject His modifications.

> God's love is meteoric, His loyalty astronomic. His purpose titanic. His verdict oceanic. Yet in His largeness nothing gets lost; Not a man, not a mouse, slips through the cracks. (Psalm 36:5–6 MSG)

No such thing as a divine dangle. God is the deliverer!

The Fix

I try to fix things and ask Him for a safety pin.
He shows me the loose ends and offers a
complete reweave.

I try to be someone's answer to prayer and
ask Him for help ...
and He shows me my lack of sufficiency,
while passing me His.

I try to prepare for and plan the future,
using my vision and resources ...
and He softly says, "Inadequate," and
readjusts my perception through His eyes.

I ask Him to change me—to make me smarter,
and wittier and prettier. And God sends
me Christ, saying:
"Here you go, Judi.
Now you've got everything you need."

> Don't become so well-adjusted to your culture that
> you fit into it without even thinking. Instead, fix
> your attention on God. You'll be changed from the
> inside/out. (Romans 12:1–2 MSG)

> Fix your eyes on Jesus. (Hebrews 12:2)

Take Courage

Can you stand strong, courageous in the face of adversity? Noah did. David did. Abraham did. *But they never did it by themselves. So why would you expect that you could?*

God deals in truth. Joshua, who had seen many battles, spoke from experience when he repeated the words God had given him: "Be strong and of good courage; do not be afraid nor be dismayed, for the Lord your God is with you wherever you go" (Joshua 1:9 NIV).

God gives pure, undiluted courage, not the watered-down version recited in some seven-step plan. When God gives, He expects you to take. David reminded his son Solomon, "Be strong and courageous and do the work. Do not be afraid or discouraged for the Lord my God will be with you" (1 Chronicles 28:20 NIV).

> But Jesus spoke to them at once. "Don't be afraid," he said. "Take courage. I am here!" (Matthew 14:27 NLT)

And He still is saying those words to you.

Crutch Theology

> Let your light shine before others, that they may see
> your good deeds and glorify the Father in heaven.
> (Matthew 5:16 NIV)

"Christianity is a crutch," someone told me—like a crutch was a bad thing. Try a broken leg without a crutch. Try finding a job without the "crutch" of education, or getting a loan without the "crutch" of good credit, or driving a car without the "crutch" of gasoline. Try forgiving someone who hurt you without the crutch of God's truth:

It's grace. God gives you something you don't deserve. It's mercy. He saves you from something you do deserve.

Check your resources. You may have everything you need for today, but tomorrow will bring on a new set of circumstances. There's always a storm brewing somewhere. But God said, "Don't fear," because He knows you have been given a crutch: The "crutch" of God's Word still supports. The "crutch" of prayer still changes lives.

The "crutch" of worship still brings us into His presence.

So take a load off. Say yes to the help, baby. You're learning to walk!

Oil

"Fret not thyself." (Psalm 37)

God's comfort is the oil you need to soften the friction in your life. *But it is practically impossible to oil a moving object.* God doesn't push us full steam ahead; He leads us down a track at a reasonable rate of speed and says, "Fret not!"

High speed has no advantage over fear and worry. "Fretting only heats the bearings, it does not generate the steam."[6] Everything operates more smoothly when cushioned by oil.

"Do not let thy bearing get hot! Let the oil of the Lord keep thee cool, lest by reason of an unholy heat thou be reckoned among evildoers."[7]

When you find yourself in the middle of locomotion, focus on your Engineer. "Your God has set you above your companions by anointing you with the oil of joy" (Psalm 45:7 KJV).

When you get back to the station, stock up on oil.

---

[6] Cowman, *Streams in the Desert.* (Grand Rapids MI, Zondervan 1996), February 15.
[7] The Silver Lining.

All-Tempa-Cheer

The little blue laundry detergent was born in the laboratories of Proctor & Gamble in 1952. They named her Cheer. These were the good old days when advertisers could use just about any superlative to describe their product. Cheer was the "Blue-Magic-Whitener" until 1960, when Cheer magically became "All-Tempa-Cheer." [8] Hot or cold water didn't matter; this stuff cleaned at every temperature.

Who can boast that kind of performance? *You—if you're a Christian.* Not just a "checkmark" Christian; an *I-personally-know-the-CEO-of-this-company* Christian. Hot or cold, you're packed and ready!

Jesus said, "I am leaving you with a gift—peace of mind and hear" (John 14:27). "He is the HOLY Spirit, who leads into all truth" (John 17:17).

God sent you a representative who teaches, counsels, prepares, and conditions you. The peace He gives you doesn't look or taste or feel like other peace. It doesn't take a clever marketing slogan to know God is *the real thing.*

Jesus already did the final wash and has offered you His kind of clean: a brand-new, fresh start—with a bonus. The Holy Spirit.

In the words of other advertising slogan geniuses, *"Get a piece of the Rock."*

---

[8]   www.cheer.com

Default

After years of dabbling in the world of typefaces, I have chosen a default font: Helvetica. It's not the frilliest, but then, neither am I. Helvetica's letters make bold statements without being brash or claiming too much territory. Helvetica is steady, strong, and dependable, and it makes what I do legible.

If you find yourself becoming tangled up in the latest and greatest trend, it's time to *reset your preset*. Protect the three most precious elements of your life: your body, your soul, and your spirit. If you haven't altered your default setting, one has been chosen for you.

Never change your settings because of somebody's version of the latest and greatest. You deserve a tested product.

When the apostle Paul wrote, "My God shall supply all your needs according to His riches in glory" (Philippians 4:19 KJV), he was speaking from experience. "The fundamental fact of existence is that this trust in God, this faith is the firm foundation under everything that makes life worth living" (Hebrews 11:1–2 MSG).

Tested. True. Legible. Accessible. Dependable. Faithful. Loving. God sent you His Son—the best.

Why would you *default* to anything else?

Dilemma

How do you get a million people and their stuff across a rushing river? Joshua had a dilemma. But he knew *a dilemma in the hands of God is an opportunity*!

Joshua reminded the people about the path God had created through the Red Sea. But Moses was gone, and they saw no visible path here. When they focused on the dilemma, they only saw the swollen, rushing, and uncrossable River Jordan. And God said, "Step into the river!" Once again, God proved He is greater than any dilemma.

Any dilemma plus God stacks the odds in your favor.

God is bigger than your problem. Holding back obstacles so you can walk firmly forward is His specialty. Breaking down large barriers is His forte.

Trust Him to do for you what He's done before. "When I am afraid I put my trust in You" (Psalm 56:3 NIV).

Now—take that step into your rushing river.

Hot or Cold?

We called the game Hot or Cold', because Treasure Hunt seemed a bit too ambitious. Our *treasures*—tarnished thimbles, gold-colored thread spools, and a variation of metal hardware—were hidden in the yard. The hider gave the seekers hints as they searched. The shout of, "Hot!" meant you were getting close, so you knew the meaning of "Cold."

God spoke to Moses from a burning bush and Elijah in a whisper inside a tornado, earthquake, and fire. Has He dropped you any hints lately?

> Whether you turn to the right or to the left, your ears will hear a voice behind you saying: "This is the way; walk in it." (Isaiah 30:21 NIV)

The contemporary translation of the Bible, *The Message*, captures Isaiah's words perfectly: "This is the right road. Walk down this road. You'll scrap your expensive and fashionable god-images. You'll throw them in the trash as so much garbage, saying, 'Good riddance.'"

Keep your eyes open to His great work. Read His Word and pray constantly and you will surely feel the warmth of His affection and the cool breeze of His comfort. Hot or cold, you're in His hands. And in His hands, it's all good.

Vision

Elisha and his servant were alone when they realized they were surrounded by the enemy army. "Don't worry about it," Elisha told the servant. "There are more on our side than on their side" (2 Kings 6:16 MSG).

Elisha and his servant prayed God would open their eyes to see truth. When they finished praying, they saw. Just beyond the enemy stood the army of the living God. God and His guys could have won Elisha's battle one knife at a-time, but in a brilliant tactical move, God closed the enemy's eyes and sent them into confusion. And another battle was won!

Just because you are visually limited doesn't mean God's army hasn't arrived. He has the vision to see and holds the power to conquer what really lies *in them-thar hills.* God is never outnumbered, outsized, or outwitted. *The army that fights for you is larger than the one that is against you.*

> So, here I am in the place of worship, eyes open, drinking in your strength and glory. In your generous love I am really living my last. My lips brim praises like fountains. I bless you every time I take a breath. My arms wave like banners of praise to you. (Psalm 63:2–4 MSG)

Falling Apart

Someone I love is falling apart, and I'm looking for a miracle. I'm out of control. (When it comes to miracles, aren't we all?)

When there seems to be no way out for you *as far as you can see,* it's time to realize, *as far as you can see isn't far enough!*

God is working totally uninfluenced by your frenzy. He has worked through other crumbled circumstances in your life.

Don't overvalue your abilities to change things with quick solutions. Don't undervalue prayer. Remember *that thing* He did for you the last time? He will do it again, His way.

Your hope should be built on nothing less.

> When doubts filled my mind, your comfort gave
> me renewed hope and cheer. (Psalm 94:19 NLT)

Sometimes when things look like they are falling apart, they are actually falling into place.

Filters

It was six in the morning; it was just God and me, the Bible, and the overture of my coffee brewer doing its giddy-up. This morning the old pot sang a different tune, spitting and coughing. I pulled the plug just in time to see squirts of steam and grounds spew from the top. The thing hissed at me! I lifted her lid to find the problem: I had forgotten to put in a filter.

When your daily grind gets a bit messy, ask yourself, *What am I using for a filter?* Take time to drip through God's promises. Then talk to Him about your day. Be sure the filter of the Holy Spirit is in place.

> He brings gifts into our lives—things like affection for others, exuberance about life, serenity. We develop a willingness to stick with things, a sense basic holiness permeates things and people. We find ourselves involved in loyal commitments, not needing to force our way in life, able to marshal and direct our energies wisely. (Galatians 5:22 MSG)

Grinding, hot water, brokenness, and loss are all part of the brewing process. Perfection comes when we are filtered by the will of the Father, with the help of the Holy Spirit.

Each day, each cup, is better than the last.

Extraordinary

Said the flour to the Baker:
"Make me into a loaf of bread.
Everyone will love me.
Mix me gently.
Knead me carefully,
and wrap me
in a warm blanket.
Put me in a loaf pan,
and watch me rise."
But the Baker, who had known the
flour as a seed, had a different plan.
"Hey," shouted the flour. "I want to
rise like the other guys!" But the Baker
was headed over to the wide-mouthed,
big-toothed silver monster!
"Trust Me," the Baker said
and dumped the flour mixture into the machine.
Even though conditions became almost
unbearable, the Baker never left the flour's side.
When the contraption's torture bell rang,
the Baker lifted the flour out; it had been
transformed, tanned,
textured, and transfigured.
The baker had made it into *a waffle*!

> He who heeds the word wisely will find good. And
> whoever trusts in the Lord, happy is he! (Proverbs
> 16:20 KJV)

God will turn your ordinary into His *extraordinary*!

Pass the syrup.

Choices

Are you having trouble making decisions? Life is not a game show, and you are not being forced to choose from three doors, so why are you feeling the pressure? You vacillate aimlessly, getting counsel from your audience, who, by the way, hasn't got any more information than you.

Yet they confidently shout out directions.

God expects you to take steps but not before contacting Him. He's much wiser than those watching you, and He loves you too much to laugh at your choices. Turning the consequences over to Him should be your first move. Wait for His direction. Moving ahead cautiously is far better than moving ahead quickly. God has the ability to look beyond and see behind roadblocks.

Ask Him to lead you. Trust Him, and be patient. God often works His greatest miracles in the waiting room. He seasons you and your solution while you are still spinning in the dilemma.

Whatever is behind the door is temporary, but your confidence in Him must be permanent!

> Have I not commanded you? Be strong and courageous. Do not be afraid; do not be discouraged, for the Lord your God will be with you wherever you go. (Joshua 1:9 NIV)

Gap Filler

God's creations shrink and swell. He works well within this process, though it may seem uncomfortable to us. He has put gaps between breaths, between bones, between steps and thoughts. Even our years written upon gravestones are measured by a gap.

Not all gaps are meant to be filled. But we try because they make us uncomfortable. Constantly filling your gaps with texts, games, apps, phone calls, and media is a synthetic fix. Instead, ask God to fill your gaps with His wisdom, courage, strength, and restoration. Then, like David, you'll be able to say, "I've thrown myself headlong into your arms. I'm celebrating your rescue. I'm singing at the top of my lungs; I'm so full of answered prayers" (Psalm 13:5–6 MSG).

> Don't fret or worry, instead of worrying, pray. Let petitions and praises shape your worries into prayers letting God know your concerns. Before you know it a sense of God's wholeness, everything coming together for good, will come and settle you down. (Philippians 4:6–7 MSG)

Make prayer your gap filler.

Glasses

When I was seven, I got glasses. I chose flair! Pink-checked Hollywood frames is what others saw when they looked at me. *But it didn't really matter what they saw, because suddenly, I saw leaves on trees, blades of grass, and facial details from five feet away.* I never knew I what I had been missing. With this new hallmark of sight, I began negotiating with God. Each morning before opening my eyes, I'd say, "Okay, God, I know You can do this. When I open my eyes, I'll see perfectly—without glasses. One, two, three …"

My eyes never got healed. But through the years, I learned being half-blind has its perks. I hardly notice dust, zits, wrinkles, or outfits that don't match. I smile at people all the time, just in case they might be smiling at me. My weak eyes blur Christmas tree lights into blooms of color, making the celebration even brighter.

If you have an unanswered prayer, never give up. But in the meantime, look at life through the eyes of your Creator. God has you right where He wants you, and even if you are not where you want to be, He is preparing what is next. Open your eyes to another wonderful day in His presence, and focus on what you have been given, not what you are missing.

> For our light and momentary troubles are achieving
> for us an eternal glory that far outweighs them all.
> (2 Corinthians 4:17 NIV)

See what He's sayin'?

Scars

Wounds rarely heal overnight. Forgiveness is big in the kingdom of God, so important that Christ included it in His example prayer: "And forgive us our sins, as we have forgiven those who sin against us" (Matthew 6:12 NLT).

You were never meant to cover your scars. But you were never meant to share the stories of your wounds with anyone who will listen either. Those are breeding grounds for bitterness.

Share your scars with God. He knows perfectly well what you're going through. But He needs your side of the story. And you need Him to hear it. From pain pours victory. When you trust Christ, the greater the obstacle course, the greater the redemption.

Don't spend one extra minute wallowing in the misery of rejection, failure, or loss. Scars are just a reference point for renewal.

And within Christ, there is always renewal.

Dilly

My guilty pleasure had become excessive. *I can stop anytime I want. I just don't want*! I would tell myself. It's not far from my house at Moose Manor to the Dairy Queen drive-through line. And a Dilly Bar is just what I need at the end of a rough day—or after dinner, or before bedtime ... So it made sense to me to order a six-pack.

The other night, I set my uneaten Dilly Bar on the kitchen counter to answer a phone call. By the time I returned, the Dilly had gone ugly. One look at the soggy wrap and decomposed Dilly, and I was rehabbed!

If you are denying an addiction, ask God to show you how it will react under adverse conditions. Then wait and wait. Ask God to reveal to you the thing He will add to your life once you've dropped the Dilly. He's got something so much better!

Ever try a Blizzard?

> God doesn't want us to be shy with His gifts, but bold and loving and sensible. (2 Timothy 1:7 MSG)

Breakfast

> Let me hear of your unfailing love each morning,
> for I am trusting you. Show me where to walk, for
> I give myself to you. (Psalm 143:8 NLT)

Some call it a morning devotional. Some call it quiet time. It's not simple to carve out these moments from your agenda, but the rest of your day depends upon it. "Seek first the kingdom of God, and all good things will be added unto you" (Matthew 6:33 KJV).

"Seek" is defined in Webster's 1828 Dictionary: "to go after to follow the primary sense is to advance, to drive forward, to press on." These precious moments you give Him are not wasted; they are invested in your day. The early moments of each day will set His work into motion. Whoever said, "Breakfast is the most important meal of the day" may not have been referring to carbs and protein

The reference may be entirely spiritual.

- Grab a portion of prayer.
- Sprinkle it with Scripture reading.
- Sip from that cup of thankfulness.
- Season the whole thing with praise.

Eat up—and experience the fullness of His direction, His counsel, His comfort, His vision, and His joy.

The snooze button cannot offer you the payoff of that first meal with God.

Borders

What started as an entertainment escape became a downward spiral called reality TV. It was innocent at first, then went radical with *Housewives* and *Hoarders*. In the triangle of "excellent, quick, and cheap" (pick two), American producers chose *quick* and *cheap*.

For a while we laughed at the overnight stardom of the unlovely, inwardly rejoicing that we weren't *that* dysfunctional. We soon learned *blowing out someone else's candle didn't make ours burn brighter.*

Meanwhile across the pond, the BBC was putting together *excellence*. Neither quick nor cheap, *Downton Abbey*, researched and well cast, hit the US of A Gangnam-Style. No warning labels were necessary, because excellence rarely panders to bottom-feeders. As goes entertainment goes society. When we lift the borders of what is acceptable, degeneration sets in, and the *new high is the new low*.

Christ put quality back into your life and expects you to exercise control over it. Refuse to be numbed by the onslaught of sex, violence, and disrespect for God's name. If you continue to dull your senses, you will miss the gift of His whisper. God gave us borders for a reason. *We don't break His rules; we break ourselves against them.*

> Without its clear guidelines for right and wrong, moral behavior would be mostly guesswork. (Romans 7:7 MSG)

Do your borders need to be defined or refined?

Heavy Load

God never designed your load to be heavy. That was your choice when you grabbed a lottery ticket, when you committed more time than you had to give, when you got yourself another credit card. Jabez cried out to the God of Israel, "Oh, that you would bless me and enlarge my territory!" (1 Chronicles 4:10 NLT).

God is abundantly capable of enlarging your territory.

But is this God's will for your life?

It took Billie Bob Harrell Jr. 20 months to lose the $31 million he won in the Texas lottery. He quit his job at Home Depot and donated to charity, including 480 turkeys to the poor. But soon his spending got out of control, and people started to harass him for money. After he separated from his wife, his son found him dead from suicide.[9]

God's perfect plan for your life is sufficiency, which is rarely found in abundance. Jesus does not give heavy loads but instead suggests, "take my yoke upon you for my yoke is easy and my burden is light." (Matthew 11:30)

> And God is able to make all grace abound to you, so that having all sufficiency in all things at all times, you may abound in every good work. (2 Corinthians 9:8 ESV)

---

[9]   www.popsugar.com/lottery

Clarity

> Anyone who intends to come with me has to let me
> lead. You're not in the driver's seat; I AM. Don't run
> from suffering; embrace it. Follow me and I'll show
> you how. Self-help is no help at all. Self-sacrifice is
> the way, my way, to finding yourself, your true self.
> (Matthew 16:24–25 MSG)

Trust the one who said, "You don't understand what I am doing"—
and you probably don't, now. Perhaps you will get it later. Or maybe
you won't, but either way you are safe with God behind the wheel.

God knows everything about you the things that hurt you, disgust
you, frustrate you, and anger you. He sees your lies and deception.
Coming clean to Him is for you own good. He set the standard.
Allow Him to forgive you so you can forgive yourself. Trust God
to do the deep cleaning, from the inside/out, so you can see more
clearly and be more clearly seen.

Just because you don't understand what He is doing right now has
never affected Him or limited His power.

Trust Him. The other side of that trust is clarity.

Gumption

It was 1865. The war between the North and South left America in an economic and emotional mess. When beloved President Abe Lincoln was murdered, the bottom dropped out.

With a wicked case of gumption, Andrew Carnegie, a Scottish American industrialist, announced his one-word solution: "Steel!" said he. "Show us!" said we. And he put his reputation and money into a steel-arched bridge across the Mississippi, boasting it was so strong an elephant could walk across it! Critics attacked him. So, Carnegie got this-here elephant, a marching band, photographers, the press, and some of his top-hatted cronies to parade across the bridge. The moment the pachyderm stepped onto the steel structure, everyone held his breath. Would it hold? They wanted it to work, for Carnegie's sake. For America's sake.[10]

Twenty-one hundred years before Carnegie, God told Jeremiah, "I'm making you as impregnable as a castle, immovable as a steel post, solid as a concrete block wall. You're a one-man defense system against this culture" (Jeremiah 1:18 MSG).

As God cared for Jeremiah and Carnegie, He cares for you. "Trust Me," He says as He steps onto the untested bridge. "Follow Me," He says and expects you to focus on the builder, not the building.

The word *gumption* has Scottish etymology, so the roots grow deep. But not as deep as the love of God. "Unfailing love," said He. "Show us," said we.

And He did.

---

[10]   PBS, *American Experience*, "Carnegie."

Habakkuk

> The Lord is my strength, and He will make my feet like hinds feet and He will make me walk on high places. (Habakkuk 3:19 KJV)

Two extra feet? This request must have seemed reasonable to a man who knew God's capacity. Habakkuk had seen the agile mountain goat's rock climbing abilities. "Hinds feet" might be just what Habakkuk needed for strength, stability, and speed, and he was not too shy to ask God for a pair. He relied upon God for every breath, every step, and every morsel of food.

When you are aspiring to high places, you are more likely to step up to ask for a job, courage, healing, protection, or purpose than "hinds feet." Miraculous is not impossible for God. But remember: He loves you enough to keep you from something that will just get in your way and cause you to stumble.

When I used to sing in front of crowds, I would get shaky nervous. One day, I changed my prayer: "Lord, don't let me sing my best—just let everyone out there think I do." He didn't laugh at the absurdity of my request: He just did it.

Take time to recognize God's work in your life!

Half-Caff

She's an exotic: skinny vanilla latte half-caff. She is no ordinary coffee. She has bigger jewelry, fancier accessories, and richer friends. Her pain results from too much tennis and exercise—not rejection. Her dilemmas, her anxiety, and her anger are all "skinny and vanilla." Not that I wish she would suffer, but I wonder, *when she suffers,* will she be prepared?

I'm a bold blend, black. Boring. But some of my finest hours of fretting to God are spent with my choice cup of coffee. I don't mask the experience with sweetener or cream (the coffee or my frets), because I know that *sipping through it all* is where I carve out precious moments with God.

Whether you're a latte or a Frappuccino, you can move forward by spending some time in the strength of His comfort. So, stay connected, and hear God say, "I will always show you where to go. I'll give you a life full in the emptiest of places—firm muscles, strong bones. You'll be like a well-watered garden, a gurgling spring that never runs dry" (Isaiah 58:11 MSG).

God loves you regardless of your beverage choice. But make sure you stir His strength into your concoction, and one day, someone may use you as an illustration: "Wouldn't you like to be just like her? She's a bold blend!"

Hedges

Why is life given to a man whose way is hidden,
whom God has hedged in? (Job 3:23 NIV)

Has God given you dark days behind the hedges? If your vision is blocked, let His spirit remind you: "This is not my final plan for you. But for now, rest behind my hedge." If you are too busy listening to the party on the other side of the fence, if you are focused upon trying to find a way out of your present situation and into theirs, you probably won't hear Him.

If you are hedged in, God is right there with you.

"Hedged in" brought Paul closer to God—in blindness and in jail, poor health, poverty, shipwrecks, and death threats. There is no space too small for God to fit, and there is no space too large for God to be found. But it's best to keep Him close. Given too much space, you may misplace Him.

God blesses those whose way is hedged in. Whatever
blocks our way may also provide for our protection.

—Frances Ridley Havergal
(1836–1879)

Heed

A wise old owl sat on an oak
The more he saw, the less he spoke.
The less he spoke, the more he heard.
Why aren't we like that wise old bird?

—English Nursery Rhyme

"Take heed," Jesus said. "Pay close attention to what you hear. The closer you listen, the more understanding you will be given—and you will receive even more." (Mark 4:24 NLT)

If you are spending listening time developing your response, you are not listening. Quick comebacks rarely provide wisdom and all too quickly float into the ether.

Listening takes time—little tastes, little swallows for good digestion.

Be like the owl: "Talk short and listen long!"

To those who listen to my teaching, more understanding will be given, and they will have an abundance of knowledge. (Matthew 13:12 NLT)

Heed.

Hold Tight

"Fiddely-hack-a-sack, you want some seafood, Mama?" My dad walked around singing this wartime song. What did it mean? (The actual words in the song are "Fododo-de-yacka saki," if it really matters.)

Dad entertained us with his version of a geriatric white-man's rap, choreographed with strange knee-jerk dance move. This was a disturbing visual to anyone not related to him. But those who knew him as Daddy, Uncle Bob, Grandpa, and Bobbob understood.

I was the child of a clown who delighted in people laughing at him. As he'd exit the room, his tune would trail off with him. *"Hold tight, hold tight, hold tight, hold tight, hold tight, Fiddely-hack-a-sack, you want some seafood, Mama?"*

Why am I sharing this lunacy so many years later? Because Dad was right. It's all about holding tight.

> For I am the Lord your God, who takes a hold of
> your right hand and says to you, "Do not fear, I will
> help you." (Isaiah 41:13 NIV)

Never let go. When things become a mess and you find yourself right smack-dab in the middle of some *"Fiddely-hack-a-sack,"* you'll need more than *"some seafood, Mama."* You need the hand of the Unclutterer.

Hold tight.

Holy Boldness

Men have an easier time with boldness than women. *Bold* isn't the choice B-word slapped on strong women—a fact that has altered my performance from time to time. I sat when I should have stood, stood when I should have walked, walked when I should have run, and let things slide way too often.

Holy boldness is different. It isn't pushy or abusive, bossy, selfish, or gender-specific.

Reverend Dudley Tyng (1825–1858) preached unrelentingly against slavery, creating much controversy in his congregation. Tyng never wavered. Speaking to more than five thousand men in what would be one of his last gusty sermons against slavery, the twenty-nine-year-old preacher said, "I would rather this right arm be amputated at the trunk than that I should come short of my duty to you in delivering God's message." A thousand men accepted Jesus Christ as their Savior that day. A short while later in a freak farming accident Tyng, only twenty-nine years old, lost his arm and lay dying. Yet, he spoke in holy boldness: "Tell everyone to stand up for Jesus."

His friend George Duffield spread Tyng's bold message by composing the words of the wonderful hymn, "Stand Up, Stand Up for Jesus."

God may not have called you to be a preacher or a song-writer, but we have all been called into holy boldness.

Hope, Luck, or Probability?

It wasn't *luck* that brought Joseph and Mary to a dirty stable for God's Son to be born. And even though young David probably was good with a slingshot, he took no chances on *probability* when he faced Goliath.

You stay in a state of anxiety for two reasons:

1. You never gave the problem to God.
2. You water down *hope* with *luck* and *probability*.

God has planned to give you *hope* and a future (Jeremiah 29:11). The Hebrew word that most accurately applies to authentic hope is *batach,* meaning to "rely upon something reliable." God knows His kids and has never broken a promise.

In 1834, Edward Mote penned these words to the hymn "Solid Rock." "My hope is built on nothing less, than Jesus' blood and righteousness."

Beyond decay, deception, and disappointment, God provides. "Jesus said: 'Anyone who listens to these words of mine and puts them into practice is like a wise man who builds his house upon the rock'" (Matthew 7:24 NIV).

My hope is built on nothing less!

Hotline

Long before the *red phone* became recognized as a link to superpowers, the hotline was in place.

Its actual beginnings go back to 1400 BC, at the birth of Adam's grandson: "And then Seth had a son whom he named Enosh. That's when men and women began praying and worshiping in the name of God" (Genesis 4:26 MSG).

For over thirty-one hundred years, we have had the ability to connect directly to the Superpower. He isn't there to jump through hoops, wave His magic wand, or give you three wishes. He's abundantly able, but His intention is to strengthen you as you walk with Him and talk to Him.

Pick up the phone. Ask Him for specifics, and thank Him for details. Then pay attention, and you will see how He is working through every circumstance of your life. For directions on how to use it, check out the words written by the apostle Paul in your manual:

> My response is to get down on my knees before the Father, this magnificent Father who parcels out all heaven and hearth. I ask Him to strengthen you by His Spirit—not a brute strength but a glorious inner strength—that Christ will live in you as you open the door and invite Him in. (Ephesians 3:14–15 MSG)

Scissorhands

Her name was Susan, and she hated me. She was bright, witty, and a natural, never needing makeup of any sort. Everyone loved her, and she seemed to love everyone. Except me. *"Personality conflict"* my mom said, paralleling some of our holiday family interactions.

Edward Scissorhands, the Pinocchio-like invention of Vincent Price's character in the 1990 movie, was temporarily given long, clipper-style scissors for fingers, while Vincent created his hands. But the creator died before he finished, and Edward was left snipping his way through life. Nobody could have any interaction with Edward, because even the most tender touch cut deeply.[11]

Is there a Scissorhands in your life? How do you cope?

Do you

- gather sympathy to build your constituency?
- alienate affection, making your friends choose sides?
- practice snappy, hurtful comebacks?

Christ's response is different. He said, "Love your enemies" (Matthew 5:44, Luke 6:27, Luke 6:35), Then, go one step further: "Pray for them"! But if your problem is a Scissorhands—stand back. God works through prayer regardless of the distance!

---

[11]   www.wikipedia.org/wiki/Edward_Scissorhands

I Lost

But God is still on the throne. I prayed my heart out for the land of the free during the 2008 presidential election. I have strong beliefs that those who can work should work. I'm not in favor of taxing the rich to pay for the poor, even having slipped out of one category into another. I choose small business as the fiber of this country, not big government.

Moral decay is far more damaging in my eyes than sugary soft drinks and table salt. And if *that* can be monitored by big government, why can't killing a child?

America didn't fall into place; it was fought into place by strong moral leaders who called right and wrong by their proper names. If your candidate won, congrats. If he or she lost, stand up, stand strong, and shout out what you believe. Get involved in a church, Bible study, and prayer group. *The land of the free exists because it is the home of the brave.* Hold your position, shake off the loss, and pray for our elected leaders and our country.

Another man's victory is not your loss; it's your opportunity. It takes more than one person to change the heart of a country, but it starts with one person. "Let there be peace on earth and let it begin in me."

> If my people who are called by my name will humble themselves and pray, and seek my face and turn from their wicked ways ... I will forgive their sin and heal their land. (2 Chronicles 7:14 NIV)

What part of that promise do you not understand?

i-Prophet

If Steve Jobs had lived longer, perhaps he would have devised some kind of personal disaster monitor, *i-Prophet,* of sorts, to give us a heads-up on what the day holds. Just charge-up the gadget and you'd be warned:

> "There's a nail in your left front tire."

> "You'll get the flu this year if you miss the shot."

> "Take side roads to work or *you'll be* the accident on GA 400."

Alas, there is no gadget that predicts or forecasts absolutes. God holds the future. He prepared each of us, whom He loved so much, when "He gave us His only Son, that whosoever believes in Him will not perish but have everlasting life" (John 3:16).

We don't need another prophet; we needed a Savior, a once-and-for-all ultimate sacrifice for the sin that has separated us from God. Christ repaired the separation we chose.

> Trust in the Lord with all your heart and lean not on your own (i-Prophet). In all your ways acknowledge Him and He shall direct your paths. (Proverbs 3:5–6)

Siri, you're toast!

Inchworm

Getting to work today, I broke all previously set records.

I took no extra time to pray for the homeless man who sleeps in the woods near my office. I gave no kind word to the sad-looking lady at the coffee drive-through and avoided all the other time-suckers—and the blessings.

Perhaps I could have learned a lesson or two from the inchworm. He does not have a fast-forward, because he is missing legs in the middle. You and I tend to ignore our middles, where our hearts sit. Matters of the heart get in the way of busyness. God has never been much of a fan of busyness, but the Master of our hearts is most assuredly is a "Middle Man."

One day that ridiculous inchworm will be a beautiful moth and will have no memory of his childhood or the cocoon he had to burst through to become what God had intended. But he will understand the importance of his middle, where his wings are now attached.

Nobody is going to remember how much time you saved this morning; but the person whose life you lifted with a smile may never forget.

> But those who wait upon the Lord shall renew
> their strength; they shall mount up with wings like
> eagles. They shall run and not be weary. They shall
> walk and not faint. (Isaiah 40:31)

Debbie Downer

She came to my house to visit. In an effort to lift her spirits, I made an assortment of *happy food—you know,* sweet and salty on frilly toothpicks! But she wanted substance, so I made her an omelet. She ate every bite, never saying a word. "Good, huh?" I prompted. Debbie nodded. Nothing I could do, nothing I could say could make Debbie happy. I had failed.

She left me with a room full of gloom to sweep up, and in the process I realized, nothing I would ever do will change Debbie for long.

I am not her Savior.

I am not the Great Physician.

I am not the Comforter.

No humor, no gifts, no brilliant quote will lift Debbie up to the place God wants her. But her visits are mood altering to me.

My grandma Clara used to say, "Choose your friends wisely because surely you will grow to be like them." I don't want to look in the mirror and see Eeyore—beyond blue. Being down only works for me when I'm on my knees, praying for God's refreshing renewal in my life and in the lives of the Debbie Downers of the world.

> A cheerful heart is good medicine, but a crushed
> spirit dries up the bones. (Proverbs 17:22 NIV)

Clay Day

Time-out would have never been an adequate punishment my two boys, who would have loved to go to their room to get away from Momma's wrath. My boys did "time in," where they were forced to sit with me for at least an hour working on an art project.

Fifty pounds of clay was schlepped from the family art room to the breakfast nook, and each kid was given a hunk of the mother lode. At best, I hoped to lead them into discussion about their bad behavior. At worst, they would hear my sermon. The clay was a distraction.

Some projects ended up under the fists of despair, but there was no giving up. *The Potter builds! The Potter corrects, mends, and perfects His creation.*

> Yet you, Lord, are our Father, we are the clay. You are the potter. We are all the work of your hand. (Isaiah 64:8 NIV)

Pinching, pulling, stretching, pounding, and carving away are an uncomfortable but necessary part of the Potter's process. It's always been God's intention to shape you into His perfect project—a chip off the old block!

Insurance

Is the policy you are holding worth the price you are paying? It's a gamble. The no-risk and low-cost insurance policy is only available in la-la land. *Risk and cost are always involved when you own something of value.* But for one exception: your life! If you have accepted Christ, you're paid in full. He absorbed the cost. He came to give, and you cannot get unless you take.

Read the policy, particularly the clause at John 3:16. See? You're covered completely!

The policy isn't based on how much you own or how much you pay, but how much He gave up in order to pay. He is God, who loved you so much, He gave His Son to pay the debt for the sin you chose in the first place.

> So, friends, we can now, without hesitation—walk right up to God, into "the Holy Place." So let's do it—full of belief, confident that we're presentable inside and out. Let's keep a firm grip on the promises that keep us going. He always keeps his word. (Hebrews 10:19, 21–22 MSG)

Integrity

Mr. Slaughter terrified me and twenty-eight other first-year design students. The first day of class, he stood before us without so much as an introduction and shouted out our first assignment.

"Using a Radiograph and eighteen-inch Strathmore board, create 360 perfectly parallel lines representing tension. If I see one line one-one hundredth out of form, you fail!" he shouted.

And he exited the room. If his intention was to make us reconsider design as a viable college major, Mr. Slaughter succeeded.

Twenty-two sleepless hours later, we hung our projects on his critique wall. "You all fail!" he screamed and mumbled something about our lack of integrity. "Same assignment every night till you get it right," he shouted and walked out of the room.

What I remember most, besides the class size-reduction by twenty-three in one week, was the term he used: *integrity*. How could a line have integrity? (Doesn't integrity have to do with moral principles and consistency?)

Integrity is an endangered species, but those who stay true are blessed by God beyond measure. "May integrity and uprightness protect me, because my hope, Lord, is in You" (Psalm 25:21 NLT).

Or in the words of Yogi Berra, "If you don't know where you are going you might end up someplace else."[12]

---

[12]   www.likesuccess.com

It Came to Pass ...

The King James Bible uses the phrase 456 times. It sounds so prophetic, doesn't it? *It came to pass.*

Two people close to me suffered for years—one as a result of choice and the other as a result of poor health. *And it came to pass.* One turned his life over to the only one who could change things. The other is still stuck between *came* and *pass.* But it ain't over.

Christians are not above difficulties. In fact, they seem to be targets. Our opponent has tailor-made schemes to thwart every good plan. Trouble will come. But when you are vested in Christ, it will *come to pass.*

The best example ever is found in Mark 16:6: "You seek Jesus of Nazareth, who was crucified. He is risen. He is not here. See the place where they laid Him."

Whether you are under the pile of problems or just standing there with a single boulder on your back, remember God has allowed that weight to strengthen you. In God's perfect time, the burden will *come to pass.*

Jericho

You're standing alone just outside the city with giants peeking over the six-by-twenty-foot walls. They're laughing at you because they know what you're going to try will be impossible. Seize the city? Everything is against you. You don't have the weapons, and by their standards, you're short.

God told His kids this land was theirs, and if they had taken Him at His word to begin with, things wouldn't have been so difficult.

Trust always depends upon action. Joshua, their leader, realized that God would do His part if the people would do their part. So, he took the step.

No matter how big your problem, God still has the power to do the impossible. His power is perfected in your weakness. Can He do it without you? Positively. He can do it alone—but you can't. Obey Him perfectly. Trust Him completely, and march forward to spectacular victory.

> Consecrate yourselves for tomorrow the Lord will
> do amazing things among you. (Joshua 3:5 NIV)

Jesus

He said, "I am The Way, the Truth and the Life. No one comes to the Father but by me" (John 14: 6).

If you are disgusted by this rigid theology, you cannot overlook His love. He has given you one gracious blessing after another. Even your worst hours are slathered with God's love, through Jesus.

> To as many as receive Him, He gives the power to become the sons of God. (1 John 1:12)

But what about "to as many as reject Him?" Until your final breath, He offers unfailing love, healing, and restoration—not conditional upon your goodness but upon His gift.

Jesus, sweet little baby in a manger, outspoken twelve-year-old in the temple, friend, healer, miracle maker—yes, all of the above. It's a wonderful story for the average human but an exceptional story of our Creator, who loved us enough to walk the earth on our behalf, fully God, fully man. *That* Jesus loves you. *That Jesus* knows you on a first-name basis.

Do you know Him?

The Whole Blessed Thing

The disciples liked what they had seen in Jesus and were interested in joining His team. But it didn't take long for them to realize He wasn't the coach they expected.

Jesus took His team to the mountain to deliver His Super Bowl speech. Instead of the "I hired you, I can fire you" lecture, He said, "Blessed are the poor in spirit for theirs is the kingdom of heaven" (Matthew 5:3–11).

Being poor is not a strong winning strategy. In a world where stuff is a good thing, more stuff is better, and the most stuff wins, Jesus says, "I love losers, and so should you."

Accumulation inspires false security and is a recipe for spiritual poverty. Jesus knew His team needed work. They were insufficient without Him. But that is where He works best!

We poor in spirit are prime for His sufficiency. From the top of a mountain to the foot of the cross, from darkness to death defeated by resurrection, it all starts with *the whole blessed thing.*

Joe

In a hole in the middle of the desert, Joe was left for dead. His brothers had finally heard enough bragging from their dad's favorite kid. Joe knew why they had dumped him into the dry well. The spoiled brat just couldn't figure out what was next. I'll bet Joseph never thought, *When I get outta this hole, I'm going to be an Egyptian big-shot, and eventually save everyone in Israel.* Whatever Joseph was imagining couldn't touch God's actual plan (Genesis 37).

Are you limiting God with your expectations? Someone pointed out to me recently that I was. "Don't put a border around God. He's bigger than that," she said.

She's right; God is completely capable of rearranging broken pieces and making them fit into His plan. Joseph was lifted from the pit and placed in a position of Egyptian leadership, never once letting go of God's hand.

If you are in a hole right now, reach up! Pray, rejoice, and trust! There is no limit to what God can do.

> Be joyful in hope, patient in affliction, faithful in prayer. (Romans 12:12 NIV)

There are blessings outside the ditch!

Love

> You might as well face it you're addicted to love.

> —Robert Palmer

Love was never intended to leave you vulnerable, suspicious, or disillusioned. But when you alter it and make yourself its beneficiary, you will always be disappointed. You give up too quickly, care more about your feelings than the feelings of others, keep score, and expose the flaws of others while you hide your own.

I know that you're doing it—because I'm doing it too.

Consider the biblical standard of love:

> Love never gives up. Love cares more for others than for self. Love doesn't want what it doesn't have. Love doesn't strut. Doesn't have a swelled head. Doesn't force itself on others. Isn't always 'me first'. Doesn't fly off the handle. Doesn't keep score of the sins of others. Doesn't revel when others grovel. Takes pleasure in the flowering of truth. Puts up with anything. Trusts God always. Always looks for the best. Never looks back but keeps going to the end. (1 Corinthians 13 MSG)

No story, no quote, no poem that has been written since can touch the standard set by God—who is love. Don't understand it? Join the club. "For now we see in a mirror dimly, but then face to face; now I know in part, but then I will know fully just as I also have been fully known. But now faith, hope, love, abide these three; but the greatest of these is love" (1 Corinthians 13:12–13).

And practice makes perfect.

Lumps

It was 1974, in China. Farmers were doing what farmers do before they plant and harvest; they find water. Neighbors had reported underground streams in the field, but nobody mentioned how difficult it would be to get a shovel through the lumpy soil. Imagine the face of the first guy who discovered the *lumps* were actually terracotta soldiers who had been buried there two thousand years earlier to keep an earthenware eye on China's first emperor. The discovery was monumental! *The lump that was the obstacle became the treasure.*

Give God your lump. In the hands of God, lumps often become building blocks.

Once you give Him charge of the excavation in your life, you must understand: discovery is just part of the process. Never give up. The lumpy field of frustration is often the place you will find your fortune. Keep digging!

> God's kingdom is like a treasure hidden in a field
> for years and then accidentally found by a trespasser.
> The finder is ecstatic—what a find!—and proceeds
> to sell everything he owns to raise money and buy
> that field. (Matthew 13:44 MSG)

Mini-sins

Did you give them the finger? Not *that one,* the one you use when the perfect you is pointing to that sinner who is doing it wrong. "They call themselves Christians, but they have that weakness."

You don't do *that thing.* You do the *church thing.* You are doing it right—for the most part. But Christ died for the whole part. "All have sinned and come short of God's glory." "All" includes you.

Sins are not catalogued by size—mini, maxi, multiple, or monumental. Sin separates us from sinless God. Don't try to justify your sins as *mini-sins* or stuff them in to a pigeonhole marked "Everybody does it." Sins that are overlooked tend to grow bigger. If you found one termite on your house, would you ignore it and walk away?

Next time you start to point the finger others who are making a mess of their lives or yours, remember your own flaws. Don't ignore your own *mini-sins,* or you may become someone else's illustration. Put your finger in your pocket along with your critical spirit.

> Rejoice in the Lord always, and again I will say it:
> Rejoice! Let your gentleness be evident to all. The
> Lord is near. (Philippians 4:4–5 NIV)

God always forgives, but it never hurts to ask yourself, *Does the one pointing that finger at me have a valid point?*

Clean

"Does this shirt look dirty?" my little boy asked me. I took a closer look and squinting, said, "Yes, I think it does." Then I quickly added, "In fact, if you have to ask, 'Does this look dirty,' the answer is always yes."

During a business meeting or two in my life, I have placed my hand strategically over a coffee drip on my jacket. Spills ruin presentation, and a cover-up is sometimes necessary. Unresolved sin stains.

The one who loves you unconditionally sees beyond the dirty shirt. He knows the depth of your soil and the stain and sent Christ to pay the price for your deep cleaning. When you give the stain to God, He immediately washes it out. Clean!

Removing God's standards from courthouses, schools, public events, and ceremonies does not loosen the boundaries of sin. Freedom to run amuck isn't freedom at all, because "amuck" stains. But God's provisional guarantee goes way beyond *clean*.

> Though your sins are like scarlet, they shall be as white as snow. (Isaiah 1:18 NIV)

Name It, Claim It

For over a year I have muddled with "name it, claim it" prayers, which incidentally work better when you know what you want. At first I struggled with lonely days, which I filled with hypotheticals. I wanted busyness. God gave me empty hours to show me how graciously He could fill them. He gave me time to pray. He gave me promises. And only when I met Him head on did I come back to the reality of His constant presence. It was here I began to understand the meaning of *name it, claim it:*

- *It* is a person.
- *His name* is God.
- *His claim* is all-sufficiency.

The one capable of taking your measly requests and turning them into His grand gestures loves you so much He would have come back just for you.

> Just think—you don't need a thing, you've got it all! All God's gifts are right in front of you as you wait expectantly for our Master Jesus to arrive on the scene for the Finale. (1 Corinthians 1:7 MSG)

The Onion

Somebody served me a big purple onion, which had been scored, salted, buttered, wrapped in foil, and baked at 350 degrees for an hour. It was delicious. The cook explained the process, and as I was scribbling down the details, I began to notice the similarities to my own life.

For over a year I have been peeling away dry, broken parts that I used to think were my protective covering. I had become *the onion*.

After the peeling came the cutting, which actually hurt worse than the peeling. But the salt hurt worst of all. Slathered with the butter of sympathy and understanding, I was bundled up on my own to face the heat.

I couldn't see what was in front of me. Matter of fact, I still can't! But I trust the cook, who knows the recipe. He wrote the book!

If you are going through the painful process of preparation, being peeled, cut, scored, buttered, and baked, thank God for each step. You are getting ready to become a delicious blessing to someone.

> Get down on your knees before the Master; it's the only way you'll get on your feet! (James 4:10 MSG)

Ping

Are you in a "ping" relationship? I have been. It takes two to play ping pong, but in the game of *ping*, there is only one active player. Using my definition, ping is a game whereby two people volley a ball and only one returns it. The volleyer waits and waits. And when the opponent (appropriately named at this point) finally decides to play, the game rules change and are redefined by his or her needs. *Ping!*

Our relationships succeed when we imitate Christ, who showed us boundaries, respect, concern, and sacrifice. It was never about what we could do for Him but what He could do *through* us.

> Love is patient and kind. Love is not jealous or boastful or proud or rude. It does not demand its own way. (1 Corinthians 13:4–5 NIV)

Love listens. Love reacts. Love puts your needs ahead of mine. And when two people work together it's a relationship. When one is doing all the work, it's just *ping*.

> If I speak with human eloquence and angelic ecstasy but don't love, I'm nothing but the creaking of a rusty gate. (1 Corinthians 13:1 MSG)

If that's the kind of relationship you are in, lay down your paddle and go home. Take your ball.

Perfect Ten

Life is one big gymnastics event. If God is your coach, you are already on the winning team. From time to time, you will flub up your floor exercise, fall off the beam, and bomb your vault. But when you stay focused upon your training, everything will come back together.

If you've been injured, you can either lay there defeated or reconnect with the Coach, who will show you, in Him, there is no defeat! "If you remain in me and I in you, you will bear much fruit; apart from me you can do nothing" (John 15:5 NIV).

Will you do it perfectly every time? Of course not. Will others criticize you when you don't? Every time! But your life isn't determined by their scores.

Paul said it best: "I can do all things through Christ who strengthens me" (Philippians 4:13).

Paul had the proof. If anyone's routine needed perfecting, his did.

Trust the Perfector!

Good Lighting

> Jesus once again addressed them: "I am the world's
> Light. No one who follows me stumbles around in
> the darkness. I provide plenty of light to live in."
> (John 8:12 MSG)

If you follow His light, you're headed in the right direction. But
if you spend your life looking for your own spotlight, you've got
a problem: the minute you step outside the spot, someone else is
certain to take your place.

If you prefer controlling the light yourself—a sort of portable "ta
dah"—you may expose yourself to some unflattering angles. If you
insist on holding the light, shine it on your face at about two o'clock.
You'll be blinded, but at least you'll look good to others. If you trust
someone else shine the light on you, don't let them lag behind you,
or you will be walking in your own shadow.

> If I make you light-bearers, you don't think I'm going
> to hide you under a bucket, do you? I'm putting you
> on a light stand. (Matthew 5:4–15 MSG)

Jesus shines within and without. When you allow Him to shine
through you, "He will direct your paths." (Proverbs 3:6 NIV) Life
is not a quest for that stand-still moment of glory in the light. It's a
matter of how you flourish in His light.

Daily Bread Crumbs

Weight Watchers introduced me to the points system. It was simple. I got twenty points a day, and each food had a point value. Apples were one point. Big Macs were fifteen. Carrots and celery were zero points. So I began counting my way through life's choices.

On a recent road trip, I reinstated the points system. Borne of boredom, I quit counting down miles and began counting up blessings:

> Starbucks signs = one point—three if I stopped.
> Dairy Queen = four points—five if I didn't stop.

I was on a roll, adding up everything from cumulous clouds to clear highways, a paid-for car, credit cards that worked, licorice candy, to XM Radio stations. As my number soared, so did my spirit. By afternoon I had accumulated so many points, it didn't bother me when traffic came to a halt. It took six firemen forty-five minutes to put out the car fire just ahead of me. I took a seven-point deduction. (My rules, my points.) The lady whose car was toast would have to claim a greater point loss, but considering that she was safe, it was a wash.

If you're dragging through the day, try the point system. Thank God for daily bread crumbs. And remember: you start fresh tomorrow. Bring with you great lessons and stories from the day before.

> God has showered you with blessings. (Psalm 116:7 MSG)

The Storm

Your storm will come,
Your storm will go,
But you have to endure
The rain, you know.

Although it looks bleak
In its vast gray form,
The sun still shines brightly
Above the storm.

You may not see it
if it's hidden from view.
It depends on whose eyes
You are seeing it through.

Your storm will come,
Your storm will go.
But it's after the storm that
The best things grow.

Poor Me

Poor Me woke up one morning, looked in the mirror, and said, "I'm sick and tired of being sick and tired."

Struggling to find answers, *Poor Me* opened her Bible at Matthew 5, where Jesus said, "Blessed are the poor in spirit, for theirs is the kingdom of heaven." God must have said these words just for her! *Poor Me* knew God loved her just the way she was, but He loved her too much to let her stay that way. With His help, she could change and step out of the darkness.

She showered, got dressed, applied a puff of perfume, and went outside her comfort zone to find somebody else who, like her, might be poor in spirit.

She didn't have to look far. For a moment, *Poor Me* forgot about her own troubles as she extended her hand down to help up the lady who was drenched in poverty and hopelessness. The lady responded, "Thank you for your help and God bless you. My name is Poor Me."

> Stoop down and reach out to those who are oppressed. Share their burdens and so complete Christ's law. If you think you are too good for that you are badly deceived. (Galatians 6:2 MSG)

Pray

Someone just called out your name and asked you to close the meeting in prayer. Your brain goes numb and you choke up, but you trip your way through the prayer, relieved to reach the *amen*. You slither from the room knowing they'll never call on you again. Your cover is blown: you're a bad pray-er.

Genuine prayer was never designed to impress but connect. If you focus upon God, you cannot lose. God loves the stutterers and the stammer-ers of uncontrived prayer. An honest petition trumps flowery words every time!

> For I will give you the right words and such wisdom
> that none of your opponents will be able to reply or
> refute you! (Luke 21:15 NLT)

Charles Swindoll writes, "We have been led to believe that in order for prayer to be effective, it must be arduous, length even painful. And we must stay at it for hours on end, pleading, longing, waiting hurting."[13] This is the very issue Jesus had with the prayers of the Jewish leaders.

When my son Christian took his first steps, he ran totally out of control. He would take a few steps, flop, stand up, and repeat the performance. Christian was doing it wrong, but he was doing it! We loved his enthusiasm.

Choose your own tempo when you pray. It's not about performance. God is more impressed by the words that come out of your heart than your mouth. When you pray, you're in the safety zone. You're talkin' to your daddy!

---

[13] Charles Swindoll, *Man to Man, page 311, Zondervan 1996*

Preggers

It's been a bad day: I'm tired and down-in-the-dumps discouraged. Midmorning, God and I figured it out:

I'm pregnant. Yep. A sixty-seven-year-old grandma! If you are a discouraged Christian—regardless of your age or sex—you are probably pregnant too.

All God's kids go through labor of one kind or another. Deliveries are neither easy nor predictable. Neither is time spent waiting. But Christians have this promise:

> Meanwhile, the moment we get tired in waiting, God's Spirit is right alongside helping us along. If we don't know how or what to pray, it doesn't matter; He does our praying in and for us, making prayer out of wordless signs our aching groans. He knows us far better than we know ourselves, knows our pregnant condition and keeps us present before God. That's why we can be so sure that every detail in our lives of love for God is worked into something good. (Romans 8:26–28 MSG)

God is just on the other side of your difficulty working things out. Carve a place for Him in your emptiness, and fill it with expectation. His gift will come in the right amount of time and is always perfect.

> Every good and perfect gift is from above, coming down from the Father of heavenly lights, who does not change like the shifting shadows. (James 1:17 NIV)

The Garden

When we started up our television/internet commercial production company, we prayed as a group for a really large job. "Just one," we asked. "You know, a catapult to success!

"God, you know we are all Christians ready for your blessing of work. Send us one really majestic television commercial production opportunity. We've seen your resume. Outstanding! Please, part the seas of the advertising agencies and let the world see how fabulous we are. Send one big cloud filled with rain." We didn't add the part about "if it is Your will," thinking that qualifier may take too many opportunities off the table. We boldly claimed God's promise to Israel in Deuteronomy 6:3: "a land abounding in milk and honey."

As we persevered, we only saw small clouds and scattered showers. Our garden would never be able to produce a large crop at this rate.

Then one day, God provided a gentle rain. It was just enough to nurture us, nothing to brag about, but nothing to drown us either. I marveled at His goodness, and was again awed by His wisdom. He knew we couldn't have handled a deluge. Not many gardens can.

> God will provide all your needs according to His riches in glory in Christ Jesus. (Philippians 4:19 KJV)

One drop at a time sustains really nice gardens. Now, go plant something.

President

I never actively sought the position of company president but always imagined it was one of honor, glory, and lavish pay. I have none of the three. I have jelly beans and problems. It's lonely at the top. There are much higher tops than my top, but it's still lonely.

Decisions must be made without emotion. Problem sharing is a thing of the past. So is vulnerability. Someone is always evaluating my ability to lead, certain they could do it better. I miss the simpler days as a kid who made stupid choices and covered them with an, "Ooops! Sorry." My parents always stood beside me as I faced the consequences and the fix.

I am alone now, but I am not an orphan. My loving, faithful heavenly Father cares about me. He will never get too old or busy to listen. He will never die. When I screw up, He is there to help me fix it. He's already paid for my consequences.

The best leader understands there is always someone who can do it better. There is no stronger advisor than God, and there is no better title than God's kid. Trumps the title of president every time.

> Be diligent to present yourself approved to God as a workman who does not need to be ashamed, accurately handling the word of truth. (2 Timothy 2:15)

Prozac

Twenty-seven years ago, my doctor prescribed Prozac to help curb my migraines. I have absolutely no idea how it works, but I'm sticking with it anyway. Please don't feed me the serotonin story. I don't understand that either. Prozac, prayer and I have had a rather productive twenty years.

I don't understand how God works either, but I'm sticking with Him anyway. He turns bad things to good for me. I love Him. He loves me more because God is love. I don't get this either.

Do I feel His presence even though I cannot see Him? Yes I do. Do I feel His peace? Absolutely. Is He the giver of perfect gifts? Will He walk me through problems? Does He have plans to prosper me? Yes, yes, and yes.

The great I Am, the Good Shepherd, Counselor, Physician, Protector, and loving Father—*that Guy*—loves me unfailingly! I don't understand it, but I will accept it every day of my life.

Can I overdose on that kind of love? I certainly hope so.

> And may you have the power to understand, as all God's people should, how wide, how long, how high, and how deep His love is. (Ephesians 3:18 NLT)

Punch and Judy

May 9, 1662: Opening night for the *Punch and Judy Puppet Show.* Crowds gather in the town square to laugh at the strange couple bash each other physically and verbally.

There is no redeeming value to *The Punch and Judy Show.* The Audience seems to get a sort of perverse pleasure seeing someone knock the stuffing out of somebody irritating, with no damage or consequence.

If this scenario sounds a bit too inviting and you find yourself dangerously close to the *bash,* step off the stage a minute. Your anger may be completely justified, but never fuel your revenge with anger.

> Lead with your ears, follow up with your tongue, and let anger straggle along in the rear. God's righteousness doesn't grow from human anger. So throw all spoiled virtue and cancerous evil in the garbage. In simple humility, let our gardener, God, landscape you with the Word, making a salvation-garden of your life. (James 1:19 MSG)

And if you should ever fall victim to Punch or Judy, remember this Psalm:

> If your heart is broken, you'll find God right there; if you're kicked in the gut, He will help you catch your breath. (Psalm 34:18 MSG)

Repairs

To save money, I decided to fix my busted sewing machine myself. How hard could it be? I began unscrewing things, looking for answers, and halfway in, I hit a stop sign: "Danger: Do not remove unless you are a certified technician." I wasn't, but how would they know? One twist later, springs and thingamabobs shot out everywhere. Gathering up all the pieces, I headed out to find a certified technician, who accepted the box of parts and sewing machine shell without saying a word (although his little smirk screamed, "Stupid woman!") Does humiliation have to be part of the apology process?

God's intention isn't to humiliate but to bring you closer to Him so He can rebuild you better than ever. Bring Him every nut, bolt, spring, and screw you've been trying to fit into your machine. Don't leave anything out. God can sort it all out, showing you which parts you need and which parts you don't.

God repairs. If you've messed up and are standing in humiliation's path, keep walking toward the Truth and Life.

> Come back to God Almighty, and He will rebuild your life, clean house of everything evil. Relax your grip on your money and abandon your gold-plated luxury. God almighty will be your treasure, more wealth than you can imagine. (Job 22:21–25 MSG)

King above Kong

The earth begins to shake. Angry smoke bellows from the mountain, and there is fire in the sky. Out of the pandemonium of hailstones, lightning, tidal waves, and hurricanes, a giant rises up. He reaches out and grabs you. You go limp in the palm of His hand, but it's not over. Gently He sets you down on top of a mountain, and in a low whisper He says, "I love you." You wonder if He sees you as lunch when you realize: *you are wearing new shoes, carrying new weapons and a shield!*

"My plans are not to harm you but to prosper you," He says, "to give you hope and a future." You look more closely at Him and realize you've been rescued by the King above Kong! This smoke-bellowing, sky-rattling, hailstone-hurling giant is your best ally.

> But me, He caught—reached all the way from sky to sea; He pulled me out of that ocean of hate, that enemy chaos, the void in which I was drowning. They hit me when I was down, but God stuck by me. He stood me up on a wide-open field. I stood there saved—surprised to be loved! (Psalm 18:16–19 MSG)

God parts your seas of separation, destroys your enemies, strengthens you in battle, and only asks that you stay close to Him so He can give you your next piece of armor and your next move. When you trust God, your rescue always comes from the *King above Kong.*

Resilience

The other day, someone told me I was resilient, which sent me off smiling. Walking away, I rehearsed the hype: "Judi stands tall and strong as she faces trials."

I liked that image. Now all I needed was a spandex outfit and satin cape so I could leap tall buildings at a single bound and boldly go where no other has gone—with pluck, bravery, and grit! In the mirror of delusion, I realize I am incapable of doing any of those things. And Spandex and I are not friends.

Hannah rejoiced: "The weapons of the strong are smashed to pieces while the weak are infused with fresh strength" (1 Samuel 2:3–5). You cannot be infused if you are unconnected. The resilience God gives is not barometric conditional or performance-based. His resilience allows you to face each situation in the full armor God provides.

God commands, "Be strong and of good courage" (Deuteronomy 31:6 MSG). If He didn't know you could pull it off, He would never have given you the direction.

Christ never rolled with the punches; He rocked the boat! Stand strong in Him. He's training us to be turn-the-other-cheekers.

Clothing is optional. Spandex versus full armor of God: your choice.

Schtick

Do you take yourself too seriously? Dr. Phil, famed television psychologist, said he had been cured from worrying about what people thought of him when his mom told him, "You would worry less about what people thought of you, if you realized how seldom they do."

Never let your mistakes define you, but use them as a reference point for how far you've come. Make them part of who you are. Learn to laugh when you stub yourself against life. Embrace your comic routine: that's your schtick!

If your mess-up goes way beyond humor, take it to the one who knows what went wrong.

> It's in Christ that we find out who we are and what we are living for. Long before we first heard of Christ and got our hopes up, He had His eye on us and had designs on us for glorious living, part of the overall purpose He is working out in everything and everyone. (Ephesians 1:11–12 MSG)

When life gets too heavy, lighten up. With humility, accept your achievements, but learn to laugh at your flops. When you are laughing at yourself, nobody can laugh at you. That is the value of schtick!

Ginormous

The word was first used by the Brits in the 1940s. Seventy-three years later, some street-smart kid educated me: "Ginormous—you know, lady, freakin' huge!" Certain the word *ginormous* would end up in the teenage bin of "Overused and Undervalued Words," I vowed never to use it. When you've got words like *humongous* and *gargantuan* who needs ginormous?

Sometimes one word is just not enough. What or who is God? One description of Him just didn't cut it for the ones who had witnessed His miracles, direction, protection, provision, compassion, and unfailing love. They felt safe in His shadow. Each time they thought they had Him pegged, He would show another dimension of His gracious, patient, comforting, ever-present, loving self. Jehovah—the one and only—said "I am El Shaddai. Walk before me and be perfect" (Genesis 17:1–2 NLT).

Eugene Peterson's modern Bible translation offers Psalm 91:1 in all its beauty: "You who sit down in the high God's presence, spend the night in Shaddai's shadow."

A single word will never fully describe God; but if ginormous is the best you can do, have at it.

I am convinced when you trust God with everything in your life, He will lift you up—*auto-magically.*

Pansy-Land

> But what happens when we live God's way? He
> brings gifts into our lives, much the same way that
> fruit appears in an orchard—things like affection
> for others, exuberance about life, serenity. (Galatians
> 5:22 MSG)

Granny Knox didn't belong to me. She was the mother of my husband's first wife, who so graciously shares her daughters and their granny with me. Granny often came to Georgia to be part of our family holidays. This sweet, rather elegant little old lady brought joy with her wherever she went.

"Coffee, Granny?" I'd ask.

"Oh yes, and one of your delicious cookies!" she'd add. Every story she told began the same: "I shall never forget …" she would say with a smile and begin her blessing recall.

When Granny Knox lost her eye to cancer and was left with an empty eye socket, she responded to sympathy by telling everyone she planned to place a pansy in the socket that once contained her eye, when the wound healed. "It would be so much prettier than a patch, don't you think?" Granny was no stranger to loss. She lost both her son and husband the same year. In response to the pity, she'd say, "The Lord surely helped me through those days."

If you are tempted to cling to the negative, step out of the pity-party into pansy-land. Your true feelings will always spill out, so make sure they are seasoned with thankfulness for what you have gotten, not anger for what you have lost. Be like Granny and pull your stories from the backside of deliverance—from the pits to *pansy-land*.

Genuine

The little shepherd boy in my nativity is a fake. It's not his fault. Blame the artist who painted him without the dirt or frays that come with his low-rung job of shepherd. When you're dealing with sheep, things get messy. And it's the shepherd's job to rescue sheep from the elements, wild animals, rushing streams, mud holes, and thorn bushes. Sheep are never safe wandering too far from the shepherd.

Are you seeing the parallel here? Do you come to the manger hiding your chips, dirt, and imperfections? You're not pulling the wool over the eyes of the Good Shepherd, who loves the you beneath the paint job. In fact, God does some of His most magnificent work with the broken and dirty!

If you have wandered into filth, if you're stuck, confused, tangled, and turned around, don't just lay there baaaaa-ing. Come to Him, just as you are. You are safe in His care. "I am the Good Shepherd. The Good Shepherd puts the sheep before himself, sacrifices himself if necessary" (John 10:11 MSG).

He's bona fide!

Slinky

The first slinky was invented in 1943, when a naval engineer dropped a steel coil down some steps: the coil traveled downward, a step at a time, and landed upright. It was mesmerizing! The engineer borrowed $500, reproduced the gadget and sold his first four hundred in a little over an hour.[14] You know, for kids! But everybody loved the contraption. It was so much more than just a toy!

College professors used Slinkys to simulate wave properties, US troops in Vietnam made mobile radio antennas from Slinky, and NASA used Slinky in space shuttle experiments. Want to make your own? Get eighty-seven feet of steel and roll it into fifty-eight perfect circles. It's that simple!

Once it's made, you can stretch it, bump it, and push it and it still holds its shape. *But be warned. It cannot be twisted.*

It's like life with Christ. No matter where you walk, the perfect circle of His love and protection surrounds you. His goodness and mercy follow you, one perfect circle after another, one day to the next. Life will bump, stretch, push, and pull you. Through it all, God still holds His shape. When you rely upon Him, you will spring back.

But be warned. He will not be twisted to fit your needs or conform to your desires. You're messing with perfection. He's so much more than just a toy! "Surely goodness and mercy shall follow me all the days of my life and I will dwell in the house of the Lord forever" (Psalm 23:6 KJV).

---

14   www.en.wikipedia.org/wiki/Slinky

Snacks 'n' Meals

"Pray without ceasing." Once again the King James translation hits a homer. The same verse's modern translation is a bit fluffier: "Be cheerful, no matter what; pray all the time; thank God no matter what happens. This is the way God wants you who belong to Christ Jesus, to live" (1 Thessalonians 5:17 MSG).

Are the prayers of the "ground grabbers" more effective than the prayers of those sitting in rush hour traffic? Not more effective necessarily—different. *Snacks 'n' meals.*

Snack praying is usually a grab and go. Tear into a prayer anytime, anyplace. Meals are more often scheduled, balanced, and not rushed. Snacks satisfy a craving. Meals require planning. Missing snacks is no biggie. Missing meals is.

Most of us are not structured enough to stick to a meal schedule. But if you only snack, you will end up on the short side of spiritual nutrition. "Pray without ceasing." It takes both snack and meals to fulfill this command.

Prayer is all about the unedited honesty of an open relationship with God. Reach out and enjoy those fragmented, sweet, salty, spontaneous snack prayers. But don't miss the meals. Take time to prepare, set up a place to dine, and reap the rewards!

Bon appetit!

The Soaps

Nothing says "soap opera" like stale organ music and an overdramatized male voiceover: "Like sands through the hourglass, so are the days of our lives."

The soaps used to be my mom's guilty pleasure. She found *The Secret Storm,* but the secret went stale when she discovered *The Edge of Night.* It all started, as it should, with *The Guiding Light.*

Soap opera fan or not, we each have appointed a *Guiding Light* in our lives. How else are we going to find our way through the *Days of our Lives?* Real life isn't predictable and is never served with canned organ music, warning us of pending disasters.

Ask yourself, "Who is my guiding light?" If you let others determine which direction you go, you will run in circles. If you have become your own *Guiding Light,* you may be the star of your own soap opera, but you have few followers.

But when you affirm God as your *Guiding Light,* you can be certain He is patient enough to pull over and wait for you when you get sidetracked. His light will never diminish or extinguish. And He loves you enough to wait.

> I will brighten the darkness before them and smooth out the road ahead of them. Yes, I will indeed do these things; I will not forsake them. (Isaiah 42:16 NLT)

Pace

My turbo Mini-Cooper has raced a Maserati on GA 400. We came in second, but the Maserati won the speeding ticket!

It's natural to want to be the top performer. But don't get ahead of God in the race. His plan is usually "slow and steady," one gear at a time.

No matter what make, model, year, or style you are, God is much more concerned by the way you are going than how fast you get there. He will never push you too hard but leads you down the road in gentle steadiness. More important to Him is the way you handle curves, bumps, detours, and dead ends. Whatever you lack, God is fully sufficient to provide.

So if you are presently stuck in a lower gear, cool your jets. Just because you come fully equipped with speed doesn't necessarily mean you are ready for it. Stay engaged. Keep your engine running smoothly. God offers *perfect peace and perfect pace.*

> Our lives get in step with God and all others by letting him set the pace, not by proudly or anxiously trying to run the parade. (Romans 3:28 MSG)

Speed Bumps

There were no parking spaces in the parking deck under Atlanta's Midtown buildings, and I was late for the first two meetings. I yelled at myself: "Find a parking place and walk, Jude". And I found a really good one.

When I came back two hours later, my car was gone. *Gone!* Standing in the place where my car had been, the dust lifted and I realized what I had done: the parking space cement marker I thought was a gift from God was actually just a speed bump. Yep! I had parked smack dab in the middle of the road, my front wheels touching a speed bump.

The garage owner scolded me, "Mahm, you pock in veddy dangerous place. They haul your car waaaaay downtown."

Metaphorically speaking, it happens to us all. When you become totally stressed out by the difficult situations in your life, you make hasty decisions based on first sight. First sight is rarely reliable because you are skipping over the wait upon the Lord principle.

Spiritual speed bumps are meant for a deep breath, prayer, and patience for direction. If you insist on trusting your quick solution and stay parked, you may face consequences that take you "waaaaaay downtown."

Remember: God is never in a hurry. Next time you are in a crazy rush, ask Him, "Is this where You want me to park, or is it just a speed bump?"

Stumbling

> The steps of the Godly are directed by the Lord. He delights in every detail of their lives; though they stumble, they will not fall; for the Lord holds them by the hand. (Psalm 37:23–24 KJV)

"When you are an old woman, you stumble," my mother-in-law told me as I tried to help her up. After two tumors had been removed from her brain stem, she was left in a fragile state. Escalators were especially frightening, so I always held her hand. (To lighten up her fear, I would rate her dismounts! She never got a perfect ten.) We both knew it was time for a walker when she began pulling us both to the ground.

If you have ever stumbled, you know the process seems to defy physics. Stumbling is always slow motion. Somewhere in between vertical and horizontal, you spot that thing that remains upright and hope it is close enough for you to grab on. In most cases, it's not.

God is the only true constant. Never let go of His hand. When you fall, He will help you up. Because He never fails. He loves the stumbler just as much as He loves the stutterer and stammerer. And He loves you at every stage of your performance.

Tape

My kids used to tape their best artwork to our refrigerator.

Each morning, I'd pick up the art that had dropped to the floor during the night and reattach it, pressing harder on the tape this time. But tape rarely holds twice.

Remember this the next time you try to fix something using what you have on hand instead of what God provides. "God, fix *my* problem with *my* tape," is never a wise request.

His solutions, blessings, and mercies are *new every morning.* Your Father is a daily bread kinda guy, who solved the world's greatest problem at the cross two thousand years ago, once and for all.

The omniscient God holds your answers, and when you're attached to Him, you're attached for good! Jesus said, "Therefore, do not worry about tomorrow, for tomorrow will worry about its own things. Sufficient for the day is its own trouble" (Matthew 6:34 KJV).

So put down your tape and step away from the solution you find easiest. Deliberately take that problem to God, and trust Him on purpose for today's fix. Repeat the words of David often: "Day and night I'll stick with God; I've got a good thing going and I'm not letting go" (Psalm 16:8 MSG).

The Task

Is there something you need to do but procrastinate away? Remember how good you felt the last time you got the thing done? As today becomes tomorrow, the stack becomes bigger and more daunting.

The gift that lies beneath the pile isn't money or fame; neither one lasts. The gift of *personal achievement* flavors your day with victory, confidence, and understanding that *the only thing bigger than you is not a thing.*

> Don't waver in resolve. Don't fear. Don't hesitate.
> Don't panic. God your God is right there with you,
> fighting with you against your enemies, fighting to
> win. (Deuteronomy 20:4 MSG)

God wants the best for your life, and if delaying the inevitable stands between you and Him, cut the distance.

Keep your eyes fixed on God as you work—
one document at a time,
    one blade of grass,
        one paint stroke,
            one sheet of drywall,
                one oil change.
Mountains are made of the stupidest stuff!

HOLY IBLE

The Bible on your shelf is safe. Dust is the only real threat—dust and neglect. Spending one's entire life on a shelf is overrated.

I opened a cabinet the other day to find four of my Bibles tucked away from sight. Aside from the dust, they were in really good condition, not like the ones I use a lot—the mobile variety that float from the kitchen to the bedroom, from the living room to the porch, to the seat of my car. These Bibles have seen suffering: tears, coffee stains, pen bleed-through, scoliosis, and dog-ears.

My first Living Bible is actually held together by gaffer's tape. Another one of the covers faintly reads: HOLY _IBLE. *That* one is my favorite. It has been said, "Bibles that are falling apart usually belong to people who aren't." I could possibly be the exception to that rule, but I can handle it. Because when I fall apart, I grab the Bible of the same description, and read the words God has for me for that day, for that situation, for that problem, for that disappointment. And in the torn and marked-up pages, He speaks to me.

The God of the shelf is the same God of the nightstand, and His Word works best in the unsafe hands of those who need Him! I am one.

> The grass withers and the flowers fade; but the Word of God stands firm forever. (Isaiah 40:8)

Protectors

My youngest son hated socks and shoes. We had plenty of discussions about their importance. He wasn't buying it so, I went to the protection angle: "You could step on a piece of glass and rip off your toe!" From that day forward, Cody wore "toe protectors." The other kids called them *shoes* but we knew better.

How can you protect yourself against something you cannot foresee? Each morning put on *protectors*—the whole armor of God—to stand firm against whatever is waiting in your path to trip you up. Paul calls them "the mighty powers of this dark world, evil spirits in heavenly places." You get the picture. You need the armor: Purposely put on each piece:

- the belt of truth
- the body armor of righteousness
- the shoes of peace
- the shield of faith
- the helmet of salvation

And once you are suited up, God gives you His great weapon, the Bible—*the sword of the Spirit.*

The enemy attacks inside/out, aiming for central control: your mind. God has given you everything you need. Put on each piece deliberately.

Hazmat suits and AK-47s don't work in this jungle. God's armor is all you need. Be strong in the Lord and in His mighty power.

You're covered!

Bouillon

Last night I served a dinner I will forever call "And Dumplings." It was a flavorless concoction of white meat and dumplings because I substituted the deep flavor of bouillon for chicken stock.

Some people are just weak, like chicken stock. They are missing the strong flavor. Some churches have the same problem.

Entertainment is no substitution for the deep flavor of the Word of God. The Holy Spirit has been given to us for a reason. He reminds us constantly that Jesus Christ is not just good history but a current event

We said "fame." He said "flavor."

We said "splash." He said "dunk."

We said "entertainment." He said "saturation."

Once and for all He came to find us, to rescue us from ourselves and our choices. He didn't pick us up by our toes and say, "Yuck, these people are a gross mess." But instead, He spread His arms wide and said, "I love you … this much!"

Choose *bouillon living* in Christ. Exchange watered-down faith for life in Christ, and become soaked in flavor.

> We can't round up enough containers to hold everything God generously pours into our lives through the Holy Spirit. (Romans 5:5 MSG)

The Why List

Could the God who turned rivers to blood, won a battle with flies, frogs, caterpillars, and hail, who made His point with disease and finally death—could *that* God have instantly transported His kids from Egypt to Canaan?

Then why didn't He?

I have a whole bunch of questions to ask when I get to glory, but the more time I spend with Him here on earth, the more I understand: I learn best in the day-by-day, step-by-step walk through the pits and the valleys.

God is there through it all and is perfectly capable of holding your problem and your hand simultaneously. No matter how wise I get, I will never fully understand. *But I will always trust Him.* All things in life pass away, but God? Never! His love becomes clearer to me each day. With every misstep and pitfall, He blesses me with something more wonderful.

It is clearer to me, now than ever: "All things work together for good for them who love God and are called according to His purpose" (Romans 8:28).

I still wonder, *Why roaches?*

The Angel

Bolting up the seemingly endless airport escalator, late for the plane, I began running the wrong way to my gate. When I caught on, I stopped dead in my tracks, did a quick 180, and charged smack-dab into this *street person.* I guess at the airport he would technically be a *Concourse B person,* but whoever he was he didn't seem to belong there. The raggedy man grabbed my arm. And the angel said unto me, "Make sure you are headed in the right direction. Then, walk."

He freaked me out, but I thanked him, shook loose of his grip, and charged off to the gate. About fifteen steps later, I glanced back. He was gone. Seriously!

The angel's words have come back to me many times since that day, to help me evaluate my mad dashes for accomplishment. I've learned the importance of "the walk." Before my first step, I try to acknowledge the fact that God is there. I invite Him to take each step and help me stay on track. Even when I mess up, He gives me a do-over. And sometimes, an *angel.*

> He ordered His angels to guard you wherever you go. If you stumble, they'll catch you. Their job is to keep you from falling. (Psalm 91:13 MSG)

The Avengers

Each one of these movie heroes is my favorite, but the best one-liners seem to come from Iron Man. His best line was delivered to the evil villain Loki, just before the final battle: "There's no version of this where you come out on top."

> Be sober-minded; be watchful. Your adversary the devil prowls around like a roaring lion, seeking someone to devour. (1 Peter 5:8)

The villain, Loki, reddish in color and blackish in heart, had horns and an evil gnarly smile. (Sound familiar?) He lurked about ready to do his damage insidiously or conspicuously but always low-down and dirty. And a handful of Avengers had trouble stopping him.

Though you are not on Team Avenger, you are constantly exposed to old black heart. He has all sorts of disguises to the right and left of evil. He may lead you into an area that delights your heart, only to later cause you cardiac trouble. Denying his existence doesn't water him down; it weakens your stand against sin.

We can't all be Avengers, but we never have to fear when we've got the ultimate Avenger, Jesus Christ, who took our sin and rose to stand beside His Father. And through Him we can face the Enemy and say, "There's no version of this where you come out on top!"

Sorry I blew the ending for ya.

Pity Party

"There is a time for everything and a season for
every activity under heaven . . . a time to weep and
a time to laugh, a time to mourn and a time to
dance," (Ecclesiastes 3:1, 4 NIV)

In order to throw a really good pity party, you need a proper setting:
a comfy chair (a bed works, but then you nod off and miss the whole
party), a blanket, a box of Kleenex, and an old black-and-white
movie. Last night's festival of tears ended up in prayer, which should
have been my first choice. Fred and Ginger brought me back to
reality as they sang and danced to Jerome Kern's tune: "Pick yourself
up, dust yourself off, start all over again."

You can only celebrate sadness for so long or it becomes a character
flaw. It was time for me to leave the party. So, I picked myself up,
dusted myself off, and headed to my Bible. I knew it would be a
fight. Few leave a good pity party of their own accord. I needed
weapons and started at Philippians 4:13, "I can do all things through
Christ who strengthens me."

God didn't make you or me to sit around feeling sorry for ourselves.
Tears are cleansing, but as Solomon points out, "for a season." Then,
"shake off your dust, rise up" (Isaiah 52:2 NIV). What is my purpose
on earth if not to show how God has worked everything out? *It
was never my intention to cram my faith down your throat but to give
witness of His goodness from mine.*

After all, how can you feel sorry for yourself when God has promised
you specifically, "Fear not, I am with you. Be not dismayed, for I am
your God. I will strengthen you and uphold you by my righteous
right hand" (Isaiah 41:10).

The Knives

Got me a set of those knives—you know, three easy payments. I wanted them quickly, so I sent in the one not-so-easy payment. These knives cut through copper pennies on TV, so you just knew they would slip through things like meat and celery.

In the hands of my teenage sons, these knives took us to a whole new dinner entertainment level. "And here, we have the rock 'n' chop," one son would announce as the other son hacked clean through a melon and screamed, "Hi-yah!"

For eight months we used and abused these tools. Then one tomato slice later, the knives that "never need sharpening," needed sharpening. "It could be a genetically tampered tomato skin," one son pointed out. But we knew the truth. The knives just *weren't cutting it* anymore.

Seems a bit like my prayer life lately. I've abused the gift of prayer, slashing here and there without much purpose.

My honing tool was Psalm 63: "Early will I seek Thee." *Everyone needs sharpening or we get lost in repetition, exchanging religion for relationship.*

Prayer is a one-on-one experience. God cuts through the most difficult situations, He is "faithful in little, faithful in much" (Luke 16:10). Trust Him with your honest requests and praise Him for what He has done, and you will be able to cut through anything.

You have the Manufacturer's guarantee!

The Lamb

She has lived with us more than thirty years. What is left of her fur is matted, her skin has thinned out, and one of her hazed-over eyes was plucked out years ago by a crazed puppy. My daughter, Kelly, and her lamb were inseparable for at least five of her thirty years. I have driven miles to retrieve the forgotten lamb. In those times of desperation, I tried to replace her, but there was no substitute.

Today I found *Lambie* in the attic on top of a heap of other stuffed animals. Although she was born beautiful, she had gotten old, frayed, and dusty. And I loved her all the more for it. The Good Shepherd loves you even more from a depth of love you will never understand. Dimmed eyes, crumbled, torn, or dirty, you will never lose value to Him. He lifts you out of a pile of others and holds you tightly, loving you all the more for your frailties.

You belong to Him. He has loved you through every compromise and failure, unaffected by your inadequacies.

If you have been pulled in all directions, squeezed too tightly, never squeezed at all, left behind, or dumped in the attic, remember: you will always be precious in His sight.

> God loves each of us as if there were only one of us.[15]
>
> —Augustine

> For by grace are you saved through faith. It is a gift of God, not of yourselves, lest anyone should boast. (Ephesians 2:8 KJV)

---

[15] www.brainyquotes.com

The Lemon

He walked the earth about five hundred years before Christ, but nobody at the time thought much of this prophet. Jeremiah was a lemon. But God had created him on purpose for *flavor*. Jeremiah carried God's message to the people of Judah:

> You have forsaken Me to worship inferior made-up gods. I AM gives you living water; and you are putting it into cracked jars. (Jeremiah 2:13 KJV)

People avoided Jeremiah like Hep C. Jeremiah the lemon could have remained in the safety of the fruit bowl; but he offered himself to God for flavor, knowing the extraction process required some pain.

If you are content sitting in the safety of the centerpiece, you will eventually become wrinkled and withered. Don't regret what you could have been if you had offered yourself to be squeezed, cut, and smashed for God's use.

He will extract wonderful flavors and bless you in the process.

Welcome the big squeeze!

The Now

> Most people let their moments sip through their fingers half-lived. They avoid the present by worrying about the future or longing for a better time and place. They forget that they are creatures who are subject to the limitations of time and space. They forget their Creator, who walks with them only in the present.[16]

If emotion and fear have begun to occupy a space of time you have yet to enter, turn your eyes to Jesus.

God is in the now. He called Himself the great I Am.

Yesterday when you made those decisions and wasted those moments, He was still the great I Am. In those dark days ahead of you, He will still be the great I Am. He is alive. He is breathing through you right now.

> Peace I leave with you; My peace I give to you; not as the world gives do I give to you. Do not let your heart be troubled, nor let it be fearful. (John 14:27 NIV)

Trust God with the reality of *the now*. Mark Twain added some of his humorous wisdom: "I am an old man and have known many troubles, but most of them never happened."[17]

---

[16] Sarah Young, *Jesus Calling, Enjoying Peace in His Presence*. (Nashville, TN: Thomas Nelson, 2004), May 1 Devotion.

[17] www.quotes/lifehack.org/quote/marktwain

The Leveler

In movies, the big weapons come out toward the end, and they call them some exotic term, like "The Finisher," or "The Leveler," or "The Jericho Missile" or "Chuck Norris."

Are you always looking for something bigger and better to wipe out (or at least verbally level) your offender? Who is more powerful than God? Isaiah saw Him clearly:

> Prepare the way of the Lord, make straight in the desert a highway for our God. Every valley shall be exalted and every mountain and hill shall be made low, the crooked straight and the rough places plain, and the glory of the Lord shall be revealed. (Isaiah 40:3–5 KJV)

Christ has leveled the playing field perfectly, so you can move forward by simply holding the hem of His garment. He adjusts your thoughts and responses to His. Even though His solutions and comebacks may not be snappy, they are abundantly sufficient for the outcome that will bring glory to Him. Imagine, being part of that!

> Live in Me. Make your home in Me, just as I do in you. In the same way that a branch can't bear grapes by itself but only by being joined to the vine, you can't bear fruit unless you are joined with Me. (John 15:4 MSG)

Prayer. It's lightweight and comes fully loaded. So pull out your *big weapon* and get into position. The battle you face is connected to His victory.

Ready, aim … pray!

The Tunnel

I have a dear friend who has just gone through another upset in her young life. She told me, "Just when I see a light at the end of the tunnel, something gets in the way."

It's easy to lose sight in the tunnel; it's dark in there. You may bump into sickness, poverty, and loss before you reach the light at the end of the tunnel. The walk through the tunnel of life has more to do with faith than sight. *Are you struggling through because you cannot see or because you do not trust?*

Jesus said, "I have come into the world as a light so that no one who believes in me should stay in darkness" (John 12:46 NIV).

That Light marches right on into the tunnel, grabs hold of your hand, and says, "Let me help you. I am the Light of the world; I'll show you the way!"

> For God who said: "Let light shine out of darkness," made His light shine in our hearts to give us the light of knowledge of God's glory that is seen in the face of Jesus Christ." (2 Corinthians 4:6 NLT)

The Lily

"This is my finest hour," said the water lily as she bloomed through the pond surface. Problem was, she didn't get a whole hour, because the day she was to make her appearance, a mudslide came crushing down on her and her dreams.

"Surely God will dig me out of this mess," said the lily. But she was in the dark for such a long time, she was sure He had forgotten her. She was discouraged. Isolation does that to a person. "Oh God," she cried, "where are you?" She closed her eyes and fell asleep in the question but was awakened by something prying her out of the ground. She hardly recognized herself—she had become ugly and hard. And the water lily said, "This is my darkest hour."

"This is my darkest hour," said the little old lady who shivered against the cold. She had run out of firewood, and her thin blankets and shawl didn't warm her. Stumbling into the night, she searched for fuel and came upon a little black rock. "A gift from God," she said. "He has blessed me with a lump of coal."

The water lily smiled. Her shining moment hadn't turned out exactly as she planned. But she had found her finest hour. And the moral to this story is: *in Christ, it is never over.*

> For we are God's masterpiece. He has created us anew in Christ Jesus so we can do the good things He planned for us long ago. (Ephesians 2:10 NLT)

The Refiner

> Jesus said, "Take heed and beware of covetousness,
> for one's life does not consist in the abundance of
> the things he possesses." He brought that home in
> some of His last earthly words to God." I want your
> will to be done, not mine." (Luke 22:42 MSG)

Jesus wasn't in search of happiness when He prayed these words;
He was about to face the agony of crucifixion as He exchanged His
life for my sin, and yours. He understood the power of His Father,
the Refiner.

For over a year, I prayed specifically, "Lord, if it would be Your will, I
would love to stay in this little country cottage I am renting." I threw
in the "if it be your will" part because I wanted to give Him a pass.

He doesn't need a pass; I need a refiner. And so do you. We need to be
cultured to understand the depth of the gifts God gives, far beyond
what we want. He sees our lives in panorama and works through us
to make the refinements.

Work hard for your dreams. Make your life count. Pray diligently for
His will in your life. Never waver. He doesn't need a pass; you need
a refiner. God holds your future gently in His very capable hands.

When it comes to jobs, healing, loss, gain, or cottages, trust God,
the Refiner, to give you His best.

Big Picture

Somebody out there is praying for a need to be met. A small amount given with the right attitude in the right place at the right time can allow you to be somebody's miracle. God doesn't need you to do it, but He knows you need the heart of a giver.

"Let others see Jesus in me" is a call to action, and the job for God's assistant is available. (Do you really want to reject *that* job offer?) Don't miss the opportunity to take part of His plan.

> Remember; a stingy planter gets a stingy crop; a lavish planter gets a lavish crop. I want each of you to take plenty of time to think it over and make up your own mind what you will give. That will protect you against sob stories and arm-twisting. God loves it when the giver delights in the giving. (2 Corinthians 9:6–7 MSG)

One day somebody may turn to you and say, "How does it feel to be the answer to my prayers?" There is no adequate response to that question. Just joy.

The Pendulum

In the gutter on the side of the road, my dad found an old wooden wall clock. My dad, a classic collector and fixer-upper, scooped up the clock and brought it home. He took out the guts of the clock, straightened, oiled, and reattached the works.

I assisted in the surgery and was still polishing the brass pendulum when dad did his, *"Ta-dah."* He gently wound the clock with the key and held it up for my approval. Like epinephrine to the heart the clock began ticking wildly in a sort of chronographic nervous breakdown. I thought it was hysterical, but Dad pointed to the pendulum in my hand and said, "Won't work without that, honey. The pendulum is the anchor and the heartbeat."

In order to keep a steady, strong beat you need the pendulum of Bible study and prayer to hold you in place.

God keeps perfect time. Make Him your pendulum.

> We who have run for our very lives to God, have every reason to grab the promised hope with both hands and never let go. (Hebrews 6:18 MSG)

Or in Dad's words, "Won't work without that, honey. The pendulum is the anchor and the heartbeat."

Chain Letter Prophecy

Here's what I read in my e-mail this morning:

> if u copy and paste this to ten people in the next ten minutes u will have the best day of ur life tomorrow. u will either get kissed or asked out. if u break this chain, u will see a little dead girl in ur room tonight. in 53 minutes someone will say "I love u' or "I'm sorry."

Frankly, I can't wait. But I'm not cutting, pasting, or passing this on, so it looks like it may have to be the little dead girl for me.

I never had the gift of prophecy, and I'm fairly certain the chain-letter e-mailer hasn't either. With no clear view of what tomorrow will bring, I'm still pretty sure I will not get kissed or asked out. Anything that involves my future is better left to the organizational skills of the one who knows me, who can see ahead and change things for the better. My future doesn't depend upon "copying and pasting to ten people." One ordinary prayer to our extraordinary God will do it.

> Keep on asking and you will receive what you asked for. Keep on seeking, and you will find. Keep on knocking and the door will be opened to you. (Matthew 7:6 MSG)

Ditch the chain letter and hit your knees. And remember: all little dead girls are alive in heaven. And they are having far too much fun up there to come down to mess up your night!

Layaway

From a retail perspective, the concept was good. The thing you have just got-to-have today won't fit into your financial buggy, so you cry, "*Layaway.*" Stake your claim, pay a bit each month, and hope the thing doesn't go out of style before you can finish paying and take it home.

> The sacrifice of Calvary was not a part-payment; it was not a partial exoneration, it was a complete and perfect payment and it obtained a complete and perfect remission of all the debts of all the believers that had lived, do live or shall live, to the very end of time.
>
> —Charles Spurgeon, April 5, 1867

God's purchasing power works like this: you cannot afford to pay for your sins. God treasured you so much, He sent His Son to earth to rescue His "must haves."

He doesn't store you on the back racks until you can afford to pay, because you never could. He gives you life on purpose and expects you to grab and excel. And because He's paid it all, there are no hefty interest charges at the end. In fact, there is no end. Christ gave it all, once and for all, so you could have it all.

Now and forever is so much better than layaway!

> Greater love has no one than this: to lay down one's life for one's friends. (John 15:13 NIV)

Stuck

God told Noah specifically how to build an ark. Noah did what God told him. He didn't try to outthink God, asking Him about the obvious problems of heat, ventilation, unhealthy air quality, or disease. Noah didn't throw out suggestions for sails or large oars. He didn't jump ahead to the "what if?" or "what then?" He simply took God at His word and did what God told him.

Have you ever been where Noah was? When the door of the ark closes behind you and you're left in the dark, how do you respond? Is your appeal a childlike whine: "Why is this happening to me?" or "When are we gonna get there?" Do you look for a way out or pout your way through the trip?

If you find yourself on a lower bunk on the ark, be brave like Noah. It may seem like you are stuck—when in fact, you're just being rescued!

> I've thrown myself headlong into your arms—I'm celebrating your *rescue*. I'm singing at the top of my lungs, I'm so full of answered prayers. (Psalm 13:5–6 MSG)

Bitterness

Bitterness is like cancer; it eats upon the host.[18]

—Maya Angelou

Anyone who has gone through hurt, loss, or rejection understands bitterness. Those who have walked through bitterness know how badly it scars.

> God's love is meteoric, His loyalty astronomic, His purpose titanic, His verdicts oceanic. Yet in His largeness nothing gets lost; not a man, not a mouse slips through the cracks. (Psalm 36:5–6 MSG)

The God of second chances handled the big stuff at the cross, so you know the taste of bitterness is temporary.

Temporary bitterness can be sweetened by learning the art of laughing at yourself. Works for me at least. God gives glory strength: "that endures the unendurable and spills over into *joy,* thanking the Father who makes us strong enough to take part in everything bright and beautiful that He has for us" (Colossians 1:12 MSG).

Don't waste your time getting in touch with your feelings; they will fool you every time. Get in touch with the facts:

> In His largeness nothing gets lost. (Psalm 36:6 MSG)

---

[18] www.thinkexist.com/quotation/bitterness

The Quilt

At ninety-two, she still cross-stitches baby quilts. "I'm not fast," Mom says, "but a little each day gets the job done." She prefers patterns with safe themes: bunnies, flowers, baby-basket Moses, Noah—you know, anything that is "precious or darling." (Her words.)

Before she sends me on errands to get new projects, she always goes through the same pre-purchase mantra: "Only buy kits with the Xs clearly marked on the cloth, and never ever get anything but pastel colors. Babies don't like bright colors." (Who knew?)

The Noah kit I brought home broke some of her rules: sienna and umber for the ark, fuchsia and chartreuse for exotic animals are apparently not *baby safe*!

I too always hoped my kids would *stay within my palette*. But eventually they became teenagers and moved over to glow-in-the-dark. By college black and white turned to gray. I longed for the day they would land the perfect khaki and navy job. They never did.

We are all a work in progress. Don't limit what He can do with what you give Him. In His hands, "All things work together for good for them who love Him and are called according to His purpose" (Romans 8:28 NLT).

Circadian Rhythm

Stumbling onto the seventeenth-floor elevator, I tripped, bumping into a lawyer friend of mine. "Sorry," I said, laughing. "Must be a hitch in my get-along."

And in his pompous, lawyer-ish way, he explained the real problem: "Your circadian rhythm is off." (I checked my blouse buttons.) He laughed his condescending, litigious laugh, then asked, "Don't you know what circadian rhythm is?" Then began his rant: "Your physical being sets up a rhythm for itself. Left-right-left-right, breathe-in, breathe-out—it's a pattern. Yours is off. Deal with it," he chided.

"Can I reverse the thing?" I asked. "You know, like waiting a split second to take another step, or holding my breath?"

"Nope," said he. *"You're pretty much stuck with it for the day."*

It's been more than twenty years since I learned about circadian rhythm. But I realize one thing for certain: there is no such thing for a Christian as the curse, *"You're pretty much stuck with it."* Prayer has become a staple in my life. Can I start the day without it? Sure. Will I wreck my car if I don't do it? Probably not. But charging into the day without praying throws me off. I need His direction, correction, and protection as I step out of my morning fog.

God will give me clarity as I need it. "All that I know now is partial and incomplete, but then I will know everything completely just as God knows me completely" (1 Corinthians 13:12).

The only thing Christians are *pretty much stuck with* is the unfailing love of God through Jesus Christ, and an opportunity for a do-over.

PUSH

Papaw was in a nursing home. Dementia was his roommate. These facilities are holding ponds for broken heroes who line the halls in their wheelchairs. If you pity them, you are no good to them; if you focus upon who they used to be, you'll both be blessed.

As I sat with my father-in-law, this nonresponsive giant, I noticed a couple comforting a man who also sat/slept outside his room. The couple kept talking to their daddy, patting and kissing his head, rubbing his shoulders, asking him to please wake up. The lady would say something funny and they both would laugh, trying to evoke some sort of response from him. But he just slept on.

I smiled at the comforters, when I noticed a large button on the man's lapel. "PUSH!" it read. (An acronym for what? Pick Up Sleazy Hitchhikers? Poor Urbanites Seek Help?)

"What does your button mean?" I asked him.

"Pray until something happens," he said. And he quoted James 5: "The effective fervent prayer of a righteous man has great power and wonderful results. Elijah was earnest when he prayed that no rain would fall for the next three years. He prayed again, this time that it would rain and down it poured."

What a great reminder for a grim time. Repetitive, proactive prayer should always be our first choice, not our last resort.

Pray Until Something Happens.

Just in Case

What is that thing in your life that seems to gnaw away at you? You've tried to control it for years, but you can't. And it's sucking the joy out of you. You're not alone. The apostle Paul called his by name. "A thorn in my side," he said. Have you turned yours over to God, or do you hold on to a little piece of it *just in case?*

God doesn't need you to be His wing man. He doesn't operate on *just in case.* And as long as you have not let go entirely, you are still holding some sort of ownership on the problem, and it all becomes a game of give and take.

God solves problems. (Think Moses.)

His plan is better than yours. (Think Elijah.)

He is more creative than you. (Think Jonah.)

God promises He will walk beside you, and He never breaks a promise. (Think Abraham).

He gives far more generously. (Think Jesus.)

Unclench your fists and open your hands.

> Didn't He keep us out of the ditch? He trained us first, passed us like silver through refining fires, brought us into hardscrabble country, pushed us to our very limit road-tested us inside an out, took us to hell and back; finally, He brought us to this well-watered place. (Psalm 66:9–12 MSG)

When you've got Christ, who could you possibly need *just in case?*

Providence

The people of Halifax, Nova Scotia built a huge theater in 1858, to fit thousands who would come to their city to hear Charles Spurgeon preach. The massive structure, quickly snapped together, would hold eight thousand; but when the great snowstorm of 1858 hit, Spurgeon himself was certain few would attend. Six thousand proved him wrong, and they worshiped all day and into the night.[19]

When the services ended and less than one hundred were left inside, one of the huge beams supporting a balcony above collapsed under the weight of the snow. Only two broken legs resulted from what could have been a catastrophe. As the people went from that place into the night, they praised God, who had blessed them with His protection. Although the snow and wind clobbered the building, they left in safety. Three hours later, the entire building collapsed.

If you trust the Holy Spirit to work in your life, you are living within His providence. Sharpen your awareness of His work in your day, praising Him beyond your circumstances. The God of the mountains is the God of the valley.

> How great is the goodness you have stored up for those who fear you. You lavish it on those who come to you for *protection*, blessing them before the watching world. (Psalm 31:19 NLT)

---

[19] "Providence," sermon #187, The Spurgeon Archive, www.spurgeon.org.

The Ripple

Walking out my front door this morning
I tripped over the hose,
that goes to the pump
that drains the pond
that overflows in the rain
that floods the basement
that ruined the floor
that cost me more than I had to fix, and …
I hurt the knee that helps me walk
to purchase new gutters
to stop the leak
that floods the pond
that needs a pump
to drain the overflow
that uses the hose
that caused the problem in the beginning.

Are you a victim of a ripple effect? As an involuntary lead character in my own comedic fairy tale, let me remind you: ripples are temporary, made for reflection, not focus.

Once the ripple starts, it's just best to ride the thing out. But as you reflect, remember God will see you through ripples just as easily as strong winds, waves, and storms. And if you want me to prove it, let me offer you an early morning vault over my pump hose.

> God's love is meteoric, His loyalty astronomic. His purpose titanic, His verdict oceanic. Yet in His largeness nothing gets lost; Not a man, not a mouse slips through the cracks. (Psalm 36:5–6 MSG)

The Rope

It extended from the rafters in the gym, a tribute to those who had scaled it. Everyone was good at something—tumbling, basketball, bars, rings … and those who weren't stood in the corner with little Billy Gates and Stevie Jobs, talking about the future. I was good at the rope. It took strength to push off from the big knot at the bottom, to climb my way to the top and clinch both the victory and the view. But as sure as you go up, you're going to have to come down.

Before you descend, you must ask yourself, *How did I get here in the first place?* If the answer is "all by myself," then you're on your own coming down. Many of those at the top find this very difficult. But if you view your gifts and achievements as having come from the Giver of perfect gifts, the descent will put you at ease.

If you understand, God attached the rope and sanctioned the climb in the first place, you can be sure He is bringing you down for a purpose. He has something else in mind, and you cannot hang on two ropes at once.

> Is there anyplace I can go to avoid your Spirit? to be out of your sight? If I climb to the sky, you're there! If I go underground, you're there! If I flew on morning's wings to the far western horizon, You'd find me in a minute— you're already there waiting! (Psalm 139:7 MSG)

The Truth

I went to an AA meeting. The wrong one. I was supposed to be at the other AA meeting for those who support fallen comrades. This group let me stay, though I was marked "an outsider." But these "insiders," from all walks of life, successes and failures, had one common bond: *Truth! Graphic, refreshing honesty!*

Some of their stories were tragic; some, redeeming. This was a lie-free zone, and I craved it. It is so much easier to love within this place of confession, where judgment is inappropriate. In truth, you turn a corner. Christ would have loved sitting in this room. He identified with truth!

In truth, life becomes tolerable, relationships become dependable, and wrongs become righted. If you have been hurt by lies, pray for the liar. Ask God to set him or her free. If he or she chooses to stay in bondage, pray even harder. In either event, it is up to you to forgive that person, "even as God through Christ has forgiven you" (Matthew 6:12).

> If you look for truth, you may find comfort in the end; if you look for comfort you will not get either comfort or truth, only soft soap and wishful thinking to begin, and in the end, despair.
>
> —C. S. Lewis

In truth, trust will grow again.

The Tune

She wasn't comfortable in crowds; but that is where she was forced to spend most of her time. Others around her were more relaxed, more confident. She was just a drop in the talent pool.

It was hard for someone of her size to carve out any personal space in a crowd. Every inch of her being was strained not to bump into the others. But they ignored her and did their own thing—humming, whistling, tapping, and tooting their own horn. She despised the cacophony.

Three taps of a wand and the chaos ceased. Silence! She braced herself when she felt the strong hand on her shoulder, knowing what came next. The pinching and pulling of her strings put a tortured strain on her, but from the pain came angelic sounds. If she had refused the touch, she would never have found her tune.

If you put yourself in the hands of the Master, He will turn anguish in your life into melodies, just like He did for *the harp*.

> Even though I walk through the darkest valley, I will fear no evil for you are with me. Your rod and your staff, they comfort me. (Psalm 23:4 NIV)

The Waitress

"I enjoyed serving you," she said. And she meant it. I spotted her in the kitchen of an Express Hotel, schlepping bananas and bacon to a makeshift buffet. Just above the nametag on her ugly uniform was the sweetest smile. *Nice countenance*, I thought.

The one-woman breakfast machine took a minute to speak to me—not to whine about the oppressive Florida heat and humidity but to give credit to the nice breeze.

"After today," she said, "I am off for three days." Then she added the "enjoyed serving you" bit. She threw her smile at me, and I caught it. I couldn't shake the thing.

The woman who worked her butt off to bring me the mediocrity of the Express Breakfast Bar, "enjoyed serving me." Sure, she had a job. But I'll bet when she was a young girl she didn't lie under a tree dreaming and saying to herself, "And when I grow up, I am going to be a waitress in a Holiday Inn breakfast bar." She deserved better, but without her, I would have had less.

Jesus Christ came to seek, serve, and save you and me, who were lost in sin. He deserved better, this suffering servant who, unlike this woman, had His eye on this job from the get-go. When you get down on your lot in life, remember the lady at the inn. She has blessed me beyond the bagel. And Christ has blessed us both beyond the cross!

> Whoever wants to be great must become a servant. Whoever wants to be first among you must be your slave. That is what the Son of Man has done. He came to serve, not to be served. (Matthew 20:28 MSG)

The Web

All who forget God—all their hopes come to nothing. They hang their life from one thin thread, they hitch their fate to a spider web. One jiggle and the thread breaks, one jab and the web collapses. (Job 8:14–15 MSG)

A spider builds overnight in intricacy, function, and speed. His masterpiece is a *yuck* to some; but to those who see the reflection of light on the silk strands, it's a *wow*!

Overnight success is also your dream. Unlike the spider, it will take you longer than overnight. Like the spider, you may get knocked down, but you get up again and start weaving. God puts together your successes and reweaves your failures for good, if you trust Him. You will never finish anything you never begin.

Don't set out each day spinning frenetically before you check the plan. Ask God to show you where to start, when to finish, and exactly what to do in the middle. Then, weave slowly and steadily.

Your accomplishment may be a *yuck* to some, but will be a *wow* to the one who shines the light on your masterpiece.

Seek the Lord and his strength; seek his presence continually! (1 Chronicles 16:11 ESV)

Standards

I belonged to a sorority for a short time in college. Not to offend, it just wasn't for me. I loved my "sisters" but I had trouble adjusting to the discrimination process for membership. Hairstyles, clothing, and who you know never mattered much to me. "We have standards," they said, but when the head of the standards committee was chosen, I realized the bar was set low.

When God carved the standards in stone, He knew in our weakness we could never fully comply. So He sent us Jesus, to show us His grace in forgiveness. The age-old standards still apply to a healthy, happy life. When we slip, intentionally or not, we have an ally— better than an ally, really, because He has the power to forgive us. But God never has said, "We'll just lower the standard so you can comply more easily." That was our idea.

God is a package deal, and the winner takes all, Father, Son, and Holy Spirit. If you choose to take what fits your own comfort level and lifestyle and leave the rest, doesn't He get the same option? If so, I hope He doesn't leave out the part where "He plans to prosper us and give us hope and a future" (Joshua 29:11).

Standards aren't negotiable. But God forgives.

The Wooden Spoon

My dear child, don't shrug off God's discipline, but
don't be crushed by it either. It's the child He loves
that He disciplines; the child He embraces, He also
corrects. (Hebrews 12:5–6 MSG)

On the wall of my mom's kitchen hung a wooden spoon with the
words "Train up a Child" carved into it. This spoon never whipped
up cakes or stirred gravy, but had been designed for … well, bigger
things. When it needed to be used, we always got the pre-spanking
mantra: "This hurts me worse than it hurts you." I always doubted it,
but I guessed parents had to say that to make themselves feel better.

The spoon has been passed on to me for my kids. More than once
I have heard my own kids say, "Oh no, she's going for the Train up
a Child!" When I stood in the place my mom stood, I recognized
the pain of punishing the child I loved. It truly did hurt me more
than them.

Discipline hurts God more than it hurts me. I recognize this from
the backside of His redemption because I cannot remember a time
in my life when God let me down. In His strength and love, He
corrects His kids. He wants the best for you and gives unfailing love.
You and I will never deserve it. But He gives it regardless, and when
we trust Him, we will never lose it.

Remember this next time you face the "Train up a Child."

The Worst

> When life is heavy and hard to take, go off by
> yourself. Enter the silence. Bow in prayer. Don't
> ask questions; Wait for hope to appear. Don't run
> from trouble. Take it full-face. The "worst" is never
> the worst. (Lamentations 3:28–30 MSG)

As a Christian, you will never experience the worst. Christ took the
worst to the cross and left it there. But how often do you wrestle with
worry in the middle of the night? "What if" are gateway words into
anxiety. Time spent worrying is time away from God.

Get on your knees and make the *Psalm 911 call.*

> All you who sit down in the high God's presence
> spend the night in Shaddai's shadow. Say this:
> God, you are my refuge. I trust in you and I'm safe!
> (Psalm 91:1 MSG)

The world's solution is to spend your days in an analyst's chair;
God's solution is to spend the night in His shadow.

Abide. (It means stay put and alert!)
   Rest.
      Trust.
         Lean.

These are quiet words that belong to the Christian who, like me,
needs to be constantly reminded: *within His presence, the worst is
never the worst.*

Because we are loved by *the best*!

U-Turns

At first Myra was irritating. She lives in my Honda navigational system and is an agonizing nag; but she sure knows how to plant me in the right direction. Myra's is big into warnings.

"In a half mile, turn right … In a quarter mile, turn right. In three hundred feet, turn right." She pushes me up to the last minute. Myra is always willing to help me correct errors. She's wicked into U-turns, which works for me when a Starbucks or Quick Trip is out of her way.

I have gotten out of God's directional pattern several times but have found that in each mess up, side trip, or distraction, He has gently shown me the next U-turn. When I take a wrong road, He tenderly says, "Take the next U-turn whenever possible." (*Whenever possible* usually means now.)

When I have gone too far, God will lovingly recalculate to another path. It may not be the one He originally chose for me, but I can be certain that because He loves me, He wants the best for me. His new route may be a little out of the way, but I am certain if I stick to the plan, I will eventually arrive at the place He intended.

Make sure God is with you as you travel. But if He says, *"Make the next U-turn,"* it would be wise for you to do it. The sooner you trust Him and obey, the sooner "He will work all things together for you for good."

"Miss"-ed

I didn't win Miss Georgia, but I did win Miss Congeniality, which means, "She's not all that pretty, but she has a nice personality."

We all want the crown and the happy ending, but God measures success differently. Slipping back is just a part of the walk to victory.

The apostle Paul had regrets. But when he finally understood who Jesus was, he was quick to admit:

> I'm not saying that I have this all together, that I have it made. But I am well on my way. Reaching out for Christ, who has so wondrously reached out for me. Friends don't get me wrong; By no means do I count myself an expert in all of this, but I've got my eye on the goal, where God is beckoning us onward—to Jesus. I'm off and running and I'm not turning back. (Philippians 3:12–14 MSG)

When you understand Jesus is Lord, the ultimate judge, you will understand: the victory He gives you is not always accompanied by a title and crown. Be careful not to put too much importance on earthly victories. You may be riding into Bethlehem on a donkey.

I didn't win Miss Georgia; but every day of my life, I hold tightly to Jesus Christ, the real prize.

And I haven't *miss*-ed a thing!

Tinker Toys

Is there a lesson to be learned from childhood toys? Playdough has taught us there is always a do-over. Barbie showed us there is more to life than looking good. And Tinker Toys taught us building up fast and cheap is not always best.

God has given you every resource you need to build your house. Maybe you've been sidetracked by "faster and fancier" ways to whip the thing together. You can never reach new heights without a solid foundation—and yours is weak.

God would never laugh at you in your insufficiency. He loved you when you began your Tinker Toy frenzy, and He will love you when you find your Tinker Toy Temple is inadequate. When the whole thing collapses, He will love you enough to scrape together what has fallen apart and build you up again, using His specifications this time, if you will let Him.

Check out your resources before you begin building. God has given you the blueprint and a direct line to Him, for any questions. The process may be slower and more painful than you expected, but trust Him with the project.

> If you believe, you will receive whatever you ask for
> in prayer. (Matthew 21:22 NIV)

Trust in the Lord with all your heart and lean not on your own Tinker Toys.

Today

"Today" is a God word. "Tomorrow" comes from Satan.[20]

—David Jeremiah

How much of today are you spending thinking about tomorrow? You call it forward thinking, but we all know it's just worry in a different wrapper.

Someone said there are 365 "fear nots" in the Bible. One for each day should cover it, but actually just one "fear not" from God should be sufficient. God can and has conquered much greater problems than yours, and not from His mighty throne in outer space; He deals with "infinity and beyond" right beside you.

> My sheep recognize My voice; I know them, and they follow Me. I give them real and eternal life. They are protected from the destroyer for good. No one can steal them out of my hand. (John 10:27–29 MSG)

In December 1859, Charles Spurgeon commented on this verse in one of his sermons: "If the truly converted man can be lost, Jesus must have meant 'lend,' when He said 'give,' 'temporary' when He said 'eternal' and 'perhaps' when He said 'never.'"

Uncertainty is the hallmark of manmade religion. Don't let tomorrow weigh you down. You're not there yet. If you are walking with Jesus, and I hope you are, ain't no GPS gonna give you such good directions. Trust Him for each day.

---

[20]   Turning Point, www.davidjeremiah.org

Tomorrow

> Even to your old age and gray hairs, I am He, I am
> He who will sustain you. I have made you and I will
> carry you; I will sustain you and I will rescue you.
> (Isaiah 46:4 NIV)

Today I am not as old as I will be tomorrow. "Old" brings loss and limitation. I'm thinking about the tomorrow that tells me, "You can no longer afford what you need—not what you want—what you need." That tomorrow may exclude good vision, hearing, and teeth. (Oh, I'll miss teeth!) That tomorrow will say, "You could have gotten good teeth if you had been smarter and saved your money." That tomorrow may reduce me to Jell-O as my food group.

Tomorrow hasn't made me any promises, because tomorrow has yet to speak!

God is the God of today—the great I Am spoke to Moses thirty-five hundred years ago. He said, "Ehyeh Asher Ehyeh: I AM, will be what I AM, will be" (Exodus 3:14).

These precious words of comfort to an impatient world still ring out to comfort you today. Don't worry about tomorrow. The I Am has it covered.

If you don't believe it, go back and read: *today.*

Training

Your greatest battle is not physical; it's spiritual, and unless you are properly trained, you will feel defeated. But in Christ, defeat is always temporary and is the place where God reaches down and reminds you again: "I can do all things through Christ who strengthens me" (Philippians 4:13).

Don't trust your interpretation of your situation. Wait for interpretation from the Holy Spirit, which involves patience and trust. Repetitively.

Take deep breaths of His Word
    Exhaust yourself in His promises
        Push on in prayer.
            Stretch yourself in praise.
            Don't skip this class.

"Whatever doesn't kill you makes you stronger." Spiritually speaking, you belong to God so nothing can kill you. Shower away the sweat, and rest away the exhaustion. But find your firm footing in Lord, and He will make you fit for the next battle.

> When my skin sags and my bones get brittle, God is
> rock-firm and faithful. (Psalm 73:26 MSG)

True Grit

Courage is being scared to death, and saddling up anyway.

—John Wayne

Riding in on a fast horse with a Colt 44 in one hand and a Winchester in the other may have been enough for Rooster Cogburn, but the disciples needed more. So do you and I. We need the boldness of God's Spirit.

True grit is an inside job. In Christ, you are locked and loaded, with a "Comforter, Helper, Intercessor, Advocate, Strengthener and Standby" (John 14:26 AMP). The Holy Spirit will change you from the inside/out. Invite Him into your life. "He will place everything true in its proper place before God; everything false He will put out with the trash to be burned" (Matthew 3:12 MSG).

Truth is the road to Christ. And on that road, God gives you the traction you need to take the hitch out of your get-along.

Occasionally you may fall off the saddle, but He will always be there to whisper, "Let Me help you up." "Be brave. Be strong. Don't give up. Expect God to get here soon" (Psalm 31:23–24 MSG).

God has given you everything in Jesus Christ, so you can say, "When I am afraid, I will saddle up anyway." That's true grit.

Sock Crisis

My dryer eats socks. They go in as a pair, but when one ends up somewhere in the dryer's digestive tract, the other sock goes into the reject bin.

> You are also to take two of each living
> creature, a male and a female, on board
> the ship, to preserve their lives with you.
> (Genesis 6:19 MSG)

Two-by-two, that's the way we like it. When you are alone, it's natural to feel like you belong in the reject bin.

> I've picked you, God says. I haven't dropped you.
> I am your partner. Everything that belongs to you
> actually belongs to me. And I take better care of
> it than you. Don't panic. I'm with you. There's
> no need to fear for I am your God. I'll give you
> strength. I'll help you. I'll hold you steady, keep a
> firm grip on you. (Isaiah 41:8–10)

If you went in as a pair but came out single, or if you never were part of a pair at all, remember: when God said He would never leave you nor forsake you, He meant it. Don't close the door of your ark too soon. God will shut the door when He is ready.

Three Dog Night got it only half-right when they sang, "One is the Loneliest Number." Perhaps they just didn't understand the power of the Holy Spirit, our partner and Comforter in every crisis—sock or otherwise.

You and He are a perfect match.

Bargain

We are God's workmanship, created for good works
in Christ. (Ephesians 2:18 ESV)

He's talkin' to you! You may be chipped and dented, but you never belonged in the markdown bin. You were no *bargain* when God created you. He knit you together in your momma's womb to become His beautiful creation.

He never intended you to be just like the others. He didn't over- or under-dose you with brains or personality. You were well thought out—every freckle, every follicle placed by God. When God paid for your sin, you were no *bargain*. He loves you, chips and all.

When you feel "not as good as," don't analyze or agonize over your imperfections. Immediately take your nicks and flaws to Him. Offer yourself to God, as David did when he said, "Soak me in your laundry and I'll come out clean. Scrub me and I'll have a snow-white life. Tune me in to foot-tapping songs, set these once broken bones to dancing" (Psalm 51:7 MSG).

He paid a high price to cover those chips and scratches.

Ba-da-bing!

That's my idea of a really good miracle—quick, neat, and showy! Ba-da-bings end up as ta-dahs. Then you can either sit back and try to explain what you did to deserve it or to cause it. Or, you can give the credit where credit is due.

When God chose a beat for you, it wasn't ba-da-bing; it was ba-bump, ba-bump. When He gave you breath, it was nothing more elaborate than in and out, or a version of that. He gave you footsteps, not wings; words, not telepathy. Every part of you was designed by God for the purpose of a relationship with Him. Ba-da-bings and ta-dahs do not strengthen any relationship.

When my life turned upside-down, I struggled with feelings of failure and rejection. There were "aha!" moments when I stepped from the fog into the light, but just when everything seemed to become clear, confusion would replace conclusion. And once again, I'd slip backward. Would there ever be an ending to this sad story? I asked God for a ba-da-bing or a ta-dah; but instead He took me for a little walk-about.

He said, "Walk with me and work with me—watch how I do it. Learn the unforced rhythms of grace" (Matthew 11:29 MSG).

God has given me time alone with Him, and the sensitivity to see Him more clearly in everything. If you are not seeing any of His ta-dahs in your life, lengthen your Bible study time and strengthen your prayers. But never fret.

You're walking with the King of the ba-da-bings!

Somebody Else's Child

For quite some time I've been praying for somebody else's child. This young, multitalented man is smart enough to know that drugs and alcohol don't pave the way to happiness. His parents, crushed by his choices, continue serving God, confident He will take care of their son. They are more concerned about their child than what other people *think* of their child, so they enlist other Christians to pray with them.

> Jesus said: "Where two or three are gathered together because of me, you can be sure that I'll be there." (Matthew 18:20 MSG)

Are you taking God at His word? The war we fight for our children is spiritual. God is in that theater, and we've got box seats to His performance. Prayer changes things, and people. God is big on audience participation but often requires us to stay in our seats while He works.

My child also has wrestled with sin, playing in the same park as my friend's child. I've run to his rescue so many times and wondered why he wouldn't squeeze into somebody else's mold. While I watched him fall short, God no doubt was watching me fall short. Being a parent is difficult.

"God will put a new song in your mouth, and many will put their trust in Him" (Psalm 40:3). Pray for God's child—the one He lends you and the one He lends somebody else. We are each somebody else's child.

Party Lines

When I was a little girl, we had a party line: one telephone line operated through a switchboard was shared by several homes, which meant anyone on your party line was privy to your conversations and you to theirs. My inquiring mind was too young to understand why Mrs. Sorensen's daughter was "in trouble," or why Mr. Knudsen had chosen a "hussy" as his secretary. But I was as certain then as I am today—nothing is safe online.

So why is it that all these years later, we still hit the phone when we have problems? Today we can connect with anyone, anywhere, anytime. But it's easy to forget the opinions and direction of friends and family are unintentionally tainted by their limited perspectives.

Your game changer is not on the other end of a line, but He's always on your circuit. Money cannot buy His wisdom. Money cannot buy His love. No form of technology will ever improve your relationship with Him.

He is waiting for your call. "Let us therefore come boldly to the throne of grace, that we may obtain mercy and find grace to help in time of need" (Hebrews 4:16).

Is there an app for that? Yep. It's prayer.

The Biscuit

Once upon a time there was a woman who couldn't afford to be fancy or skilled or skinny. Poverty was her only stain. She worked with what she had: soap and water, self-rising flour, buttermilk, a broom, a bed, and a Bible.

People had tried to teach her to be prosperous, but she was no fit for their style of life. She had everything she ever needed in Jesus, who provided a broom, a bed, a Bible, and a biscuit. The Bible sustained beyond the biscuit, and although the biscuit was her idea of perfection in daily bread, she knew the words of Jesus: "You cannot live by bread alone."

She valued her broom because she had read, "He is going to clean house—make a clean sweep of your lives" (Matthew 3:12 MSG).

Her bed fit her perfectly. "Don't you know He enjoys giving rest to those He loves?" (Psalm 127:2 MSG).

You might be able to improve her life, but she would probably do better improving yours. Her joy is in the Lord, who sweeps her problems away, gives rest, and blesses her beyond the biscuit.

She has His Word on it!

Regrets

Clutch your pillow to your head,
Remember all the words you said.
Think of drama, think of dread,
Once again ... it stings.
Hit your knees and turn instead
To the one who gives the bread.
Give your Dad the *go-ahead*
To heal broken things.

Praise the God of second chances. It has never been His intention to leave you in the ditch. If you have been there for a while, ask yourself, *Am I emotionally stuck here, or is God working through me for a greater purpose?*

> The righteous person faces many troubles, but the Lord comes to the rescue each time. (Psalm 34:19 NLT)

If you are calling out from the ditch, you are doing it right. Call out! Regardless of how you got there, the Father was right there with you when you fell in. If you didn't see Him, you weren't focused, which may be the reason you slipped in the first place. Give Him your regrets, and He will show you healing of His forgiveness and the wonders of His love.

He heals broken things.

Miracles

God has rescued me from impossible situations using outrageous solutions. And beyond the rescue, He brought me to the land of milk and honey. (Actually it was a cottage, with a peach and apple tree, which was just as good to me!)

God is my story. His blessings don't make sense to me. Neither do stiletto heels, aviation, or computer code, but I have depended upon each. It is not my job to explain God, just to follow Him. He leads me. I don't want to turn away, because I don't want to get where I'm going only to notice He isn't there.

Is God capable of keeping a man safe in the stomach of a fish? How about rescuing a family from a flood that covers the earth? Can He deliver you from the anguish of a loss of a loved one or the distress of losing a home or a job? How about all three at once? Yeah, that'll happen when the Red Sea parts.

David wrote, "I said to myself, 'relax and rest. God has showered you with blessings. Soul, you've been rescued from death; Eye, you've been rescued from tears. And you, Foot, were kept from stumbling" (Psalm 116:7–8 MSG).

It's not just a story. It's not just a myth. It's a miracle!

The Hit

When you get the news, it's shattering. You've been let go. Terminated. Dumped. Foreclosed on. It all means the same thing: It's over.

You forget how to breathe. "In and out," you remind yourself, but you don't trust your autopilot. The author of confusion has written you into his story. Then, you remember: you are not part of his story—you don't belong to him.

You belong to the one who said, "I will never leave you nor forsake you," and "I am with always, even unto the ends of the earth." It's not the end of the earth, of course, even though it feels like it. But God's love never fails. He stays with you in, through, and beyond the worse circumstance.

As the days go by, as you trust Him fully, He pieces your life back together again, and you see purpose. The words that wounded you so can only hurt you as long as you let them. And they will never impact your life more than the words written two thousand years ago:

> For I am convinced that neither death nor life, neither angels nor demons, neither the present nor the future, nor any powers, neither height nor depth, nor anything else in all creation will be able to separate us from the love of God that is in Christ Jesus our Lord. (Romans 8:38)

> It ain't about how hard you hit. It's about how hard you can get hit, how much you can take and keep moving forward.[21]

---

[21] Rocky Balboa, Rocky, United Artists, 1976, John G. Avildsen, director, Sylvester Stallone, Writer.

Truffles

If I had been the first one to find a truffle, I'd have left it alone. It looks like something out of an oncology textbook. Wikipedia tells me truffles are fungus. A really expensive fungus! White truffles go for as much as $3,600 a pound.[22] Hats off to whoever was brave enough to figure out the "amazing flavor and aroma" thing. It wouldn't have been me.

Truffles live in dark and dirty places, crammed near tree roots. In France, they are foraged out of the ground by pigs. Once you pry them out of the pig's mouth, you must scrub them, shave them, grind, and puree them. And voila! This fungal pig food is magically transformed into what chefs call white gold—the diamond of the kitchen.

Have you been discovered yet, or are you sitting in the dark, untouched and wondering if only pigs know where to find you?

If you feel lost, be thankful. "The Son of man is come to seek and to save that which was lost" (Luke 19:10 KJV). He knows right where to find you. Allow yourself to be used for His purpose, to be dug out, scrubbed, shaved, ground, and pureed. He paid a high price for you, and you are precious in His sight.

---

[22] *Truffles: The Most Expensive Food in the World*, CBS News, Lesley Stahl, June 4, 2012.

Wrestling

Jacob was alone in the desert. He had sent his women and children to soften the heart of Esau, the brother he had cheated so many years ago. Alone in the desert, Jacob was left to evaluate himself: This liar and cheater had turned chicken.

Alone in the desert, Jacob fell into a fitful sleep, and there he met the Angel of God (Genesis 32). At the point most of us would have cowered and begged for mercy, Jacob took the Angel of God into the ring to remind God of His promise. Jacob wrestled. And he kept wrestling until the Angel agreed once again to bless Jacob. My sense of justice tells me Jacob deserved a slap on his fake fur hand. But justice isn't mine.

When you are caught in sin, don't keep running. Stand still, in the shadow of God Almighty, and confess. The sin can never be taken from you any other way. Spend some time with Him, even if it requires wrestling with His promises.

The night Jacob wrestled with the Angel of God, he came away with two things: a blessing from God and a limp. But it's better to limp away forgiven and blessed than to walk away empty-handed.

> With all my heart, I want your blessings. Be merciful
> as you promised. (Psalm 119:58 NLT)

Spokes and Cloth

Monday morning, New York City: Rain blew sideways, turning umbrellas into weapons. By afternoon, the city street corner trash cans were stuffed with blown-out umbrella carcasses. (Why repair an item that can be replaced for only "two dollah" at a corner bodega?)

Spokes and cloth won't hold up in a storm. Neither will bank accounts, 401Ks, a Mercedes Benz, or country-club living. Your reputation is only as safe as your last transaction. Your level of education is only as important as someone makes it. It's all *spokes and cloth.*

Whatever protects you one moment can often end up inside-out, the next. There is only one safe hiding place in the storm, and the cost was far greater than two dollah.

Shortly before He was crucified Jesus told His disciples, "Right now I am storm-tossed. And what am I going to say? 'Father get me out of this?' No, this is why I came in the first place. I'll say, 'Father, put your glory on display." A voice came out of the sky: 'I have glorified it, and I'll glorify it again" (John 12:27–28 MSG)

Jesus Christ has been sent to rescue you from the storms that twist and tear spokes and cloth. Trust His Word. "It will be shelter and shade from the heat of the day and a refuge and hiding place from the storm and rain" (Isaiah 4:6 NIV).

Myopia

> Why did Simon Peter doubt? He doubted for two reasons; First, because he looked too much to second causes, and secondly because he looked too little at the first cause.
>
> —Charles Spurgeon 1859

Perhaps the Disciple Peter was myopic, like me. Back then there was no eye test to determine visual limitations.

When I learned to water-ski, I left my Coke bottle–thick bifocal glasses on shore and trusted my driver to lead me in the paths of no tree stumps or other boats. Everything was a blur skimming across Lake Lanier; but I wasn't there for the view. I was conquering the pond!

Then God had one of His guys invent contact lenses, and my world became clearer and more joyful. My lenses and I headed back to the water; but this time water skiing didn't go so well. I had trouble getting up. I had trouble staying up. And my falls were *agony-of-defeat dramatic*!

Like Peter, I had focused on the secondary view, taking my eyes of my primary goal. Running blind is not a bad thing if you have faith. But nothing trips up faith like distractions. No matter how far or well you see, never let the waves or the view distract you. "If I keep my eyes on God, I won't trip over my own feet" (Psalm 25:15 MSG).

The Lesson of Wait

On a clear day, you can see "Old Yella" coming up the hill. My kids and I spent many mornings on the street corner waiting for the school bus. In boredom and frustration, we created the School-Bus Waiting Game.

"In fifteen more cars," I began, "the school bus will be here." After the failed count, each kid would call out his or her numerical guess. Nobody ever got it right. The bus came when it came, and until then, we waited.

Moses learned the value of the lesson of waiting when God called him to the mountain for a one-on-one (Exodus 24:12–18). But during the hike to the top, the mountaintop got socked-in with fog. (The top often is.) God had called Moses, and Moses would wait there, not until the fog lifted, not for the ta-dah moment, but until he met God. And seven days later, God appeared. *Glowingly. In time and on purpose.*

If you give God time, He will show you His plan for you. He is actually in that fog with you right this minute. Keep your eyes open.

He will always show up. *Glowingly. In time and on purpose.*

Roots

Bradford pear trees have gotten a bad rap. Is it their fault? We chose them because we knew they grew big and beautiful quickly. We loved their shape and their blossoms. Their tree roots were shallow, but nobody could see the roots, so what did it matter? Then after one strong summer rain, "big, branchy, and beautiful" became "bent and broken."

This is your fate if you neglect your root system. What a blessing you will be if you spread your branches to bless the world with your beauty. But remember: you need a strong root system to support all that radiance. Or one rainstorm later, you're firewood.

If you want to be healthy and withstand storms, you've got to check your owner's manual. Within that manual you will find the Arborist's guarantee. Give Him the time and opportunity, and He will strengthen your growth.

You may never be as tall and beautiful as the tree next door, but you know your strength lies beyond the foliage.

Others may not understand why you stand strong, but they will certainly notice that you stand strong when the winds hit.

Growing up and out only works when you have first *grown deep*. Trust God's gardening techniques: "And you will be like a tree planted by the rivers of water … whose leaf does not wither. Whatsoever you do, you will prosper" (Psalm 1:3 KJV).

Under the Cloud

Under the cloud, you cannot see the sun.
Under the cloud, you cannot focus clearly.
Under the cloud, colors are diminished.
So why would you want to live there?

Remaining *under the cloud* is a choice. We've all visited that space from time to time, and we may be back. But we were never meant to live there.

God blesses us in these temporary places. Rain makes things grow. But we were never made to live in the negative. Why would you choose to stay there? The party He has planned for you is so much greater than the pity party you have chosen. Remember these words: "May the God of hope fill you will all joy and peace as you trust in Him, so that you may overflow with hope by the power of the Holy Spirit" (Romans 15:13).

Under the cloud, you have very little to give. Under the cloud inspiration is lost, and you have very little to give anyone else. Because, under the cloud, it's only about you. Come out, come out, wherever you are, into the joy of God's fullness.

> Let your light shine before others that they may see
> the good things you do, and glorify your Father in
> heaven. (Matthew 5:16)

Salt and Light

The doctor said I had a sinus infection: "Salt and light—that's what you need. Works on pretty much any infection." He clarified: "Use a saltwater neti pot and get out in the sun." I had heard this before only not much as what I needed to use as what I needed to be.

Jesus said, "Let me tell you why you are here. You're here to bring out the God-flavors of this earth. If you lose your saltiness, how will people taste godliness? You've lost your usefulness and will end up in the garbage. Here's another way to put it: you're here to be a light, bringing out the God-colors in the world. God is not a secret to be kept" (Matthew 5:13–15 MSG).

"You are the light of the world," Jesus said (Matthew 5:14 NIV). It's not a suggestion; it's a charge. God blesses the one who has the gumption to step out of the darkness into the light. Bring your empty salt shaker to Him, and let Him fill you with His seasoning. Step out of the darkness into His clarity.

Salt and light, *"works pretty much on any infection."*

The Whine

For thirty-eight years he had suffered alone. There was no clinic, pain meds, or advocate. Somehow he dragged himself to the Bethesda Pool in Jerusalem, where the paralyzed, blind, and sick had been healed. He lay beside the pool, hoping to jump in when the waters stirred. The first one into the moving water was always healed. But the younger ones and the ones who had help had beaten him to the blessing every time.

Jesus came looking for the man. (He does that when we're despondent, discouraged, troubled, and in pain). And Jesus asked him, "Do you want to get well?" The man whined, "I've been sick for years, and now I'm laying here unable to drag myself into the water. Nobody is willing to help me. I'll never get healed" (John 5).

Jesus had come to heal the man, not listen to his whine. But Jesus listened anyway. (He does that when we're despondent, discouraged, troubled, and in pain.)

Then Jesus said, "Pick up your mat and walk." Thirty-eight years and one day later, the man walked. He overlooked the obstacles and disregarded reason as he focused upon Jesus, who had simply asked him, "Do you want to get well?"

How about you—do you want to get well? If you are lambasted with difficulties, James 1 says, "Consider it pure joy."

But in order to hold the joy, you have to drop the whine.

Mundane

Are you doing something significant with your life? Will there be a discovery or invention to name after you when you go, or do you feel like you're just a drop in the talent pool? If you consider your job mundane, look again:

"Oh, ye dude-of-recliner-and-beer …"

"Oh, ye dudette-of-sofa-and-Chablis …"

God has so much more in store for you. He never sent His Son to rescue you just so you could live your life in mediocrity. He came after you because He believes you are worth it.

"God don't make junk."[23] If you feel like you are just a waste of His creation, you have got it so wrong. Jesus said, "You're tied down to the mundane. I'm in touch with what is beyond your horizons. You live in terms of what you see and touch. I'm living on other terms. I told you that you were missing God in all this. You're at a dead-end. If you won't believe I am who I say I am you are at the dead-end of sins. You're missing God in your lives" (John 8:23–24 MSG).

Can you see God from where you are standing or sitting? He is there. God will make a masterpiece out of your mundane life if you are willing to take the steps He asks you to take. Put down the remote and step away from the recliner. Now repeat after me: *change me, Lord.*

God can do miracles without you, but He wants to include you. How's that for significance!

---

[23] www.meetville.com/ethelwatersquotes

Infinity and Beyond!

Ever ask a kid to draw God? It's pretty amazing stuff. Ever ask an adult to explain who God is to them? Even more amazing.

Biblical references are varied, not for His purpose but for our purpose of understanding. One hundred and two different attributes are just the tip of the iceberg.

God knows the ins and outs of lions' dens, furnaces, and fish bellies. God is too magnificent for explanation, as evidenced by the way He explained who He was to Moses: "I AM WHO I AM" (Exodus 3:14 MSG).

Every breath I take draws me closer to my final one on earth. I don't count but freely inhale and exhale as I desire. Every moment, I Am is with me. Tomorrow, the great I Am will still be the great I Am. He was not the great I Was yesterday and is not the great I Will Be tomorrow.

I Am sums it up. I Am conquered death from sin and holds the promise of eternal life through Jesus Christ. He has broken the boundaries of the next minute. *I Am* is already there.

How long can you rely on Him? That which is hard for us to comprehend is rather easily explained by a toy astronaut named Buzz Lightyear: "To infinity and beyond!"

Wobbling

The bride glides down the aisle bogged down with yards of tulle and lace pinned to her head, and *something old, something new, something borrowed, and something blue.* Everyone watches her measured steps.

She is not used to this slow pace. Just last week she was running from around in the typical pre-wedding frenzy. But today, she must walk slowly with her eye on the prize. *Slow* is a foreign concept to her. *She wobbles.*

Slow is a foreign concept to us. *We wobble.* Try it. Slowly hum, "Here Comes the Bride," and in small, slow steps walk, without wobbling. Hard, huh?

Walking slowly is more about balance than distance.

Ask God to direct your steps and you will cover much greater territory, more efficiently and productively.

> But those who wait upon the Lord get fresh strength. They spread their wings and soar like eagles. They run and don't get tired. They walk and don't lag behind. (Isaiah 40:31 MSG)

The Lord respects a good wobble—and He loves the wobbler.

Cracks

I've been trying to find a material that will fill in a gap in a butcher-block table. The thing leaks when I cut watermelon on it. I've tried a few products to repair the crack, but they're all synthetic. I need organic—you know, the stuff that breathes, shrinks, and swells. Like wood. Like me. Like you.

Jesus said, "If you love me, keep my commands, and I will ask the Father to give you another Comforter, that He may abide with you forever" (John 14:16 KJV). He knew we couldn't do it on our own, So He sent the third part of the Trinity to strengthen, support, sensitize, and sustain. The Holy Spirit is the real deal, who breathes life into us to fill the shrunken, swollen, and cracked places. He's authentic. No artificial faux bois stuff. He's organic!

Don't take His presence lightly. When you accepted the Father and Son, you received the Holy Spirit. Don't overlook the gift.

> May the God of hope fill you all with joy and peace as you trust in Him, so that you may overflow with the hope by the power of the Holy Spirit. (Romans 15:13 NIV)

> I will lead the blind by ways they have not known, along unfamiliar paths I will guide them; I will turn the darkness into light before them and make the *rough places* smooth. These are the things I will do; I will not forsake them. (Isaiah 42:16 NIV)

Get filled!

You Alone?

Me too. Visibly.
But beyond my visibility,
I'm surrounded, by the power
of One. God is working in
around and through me.
Because I asked Him.
Because I trust Him.
Because I give Him time.
It's a deliberate action.

Twenty-six thousand Chinese have spent years building the world's largest dam to hold back the Yangtze River. They have already gone through $25 billion, and it's still not complete. You have got to wonder how much prayer was involved in the process. How many of the builders or their families contacted the *Force of One,* who could hold back the Yangtze single-handedly?

One parted the sea in a night.

One inspired a jailbird to write a large part of the Bible.

And One has done magnificent things in the life of one of His weakest kids. That's me.

One keeps me company.

You alone?
Your candle burns brighter
in the dark. And that's where
He shows you miracles in your life.
Because you ask Him
Because you trust Him
Because you give Him time.
Because He loves you!

Deadwood

I had coffee with a lady who was full of regret for something she had done. Counseling had given her the right words of explanation and extrication. But I could see from her tears, she wasn't buying it. She kept bringing the mistake she had made yesterday to today's table.

God had forgiven her. The bill had been paid. But she was still loaded down with deadwood, which left her no room to carry anything else.

It's not a numbers game. One rotten deed doesn't wipe out a good one, and vice versa. The Lord loves the child who messes up. Every mistake, miscalculation, and misstep requires accountability. Then, take it to the cross, lay it down, and walk away. *God has forgiven you that sin. He let it go, and you must too!* When you give it to Him, He works your life for His good. Promise! (His, not mine.)

Your life is a symphony of highs and lows, loud and soft tones, which can only be orchestrated by God. So don't dwell on the disappointment or spend one minute longer lamenting over what He has already forgiven. He will turn things around for you if you trust Him. You are God's progressive revelation. You're in training!

Drop the deadwood at the cross.

> What counts is your life. Is it green and blossoming?
> Because if it's deadwood, it goes on the fire.
> (Matthew 3:10 MSG)

Lottery

I only bought one ticket, but as my nephew pointed out, if God intended for me to win, one would do it. He didn't. I was one of the 175 million losers.

In 2011, a single mom won $5 million of the Georgia lottery. From the $1.3 million left after taxes, she bought a new wardrobe at the Salvation Army Store. She cut four jobs back to one and invested the rest of her money. Then came the calls from her "new friends," investment counselors, the sick, the poor, the needy, and those with great financial opportunities. She got marriage proposals and threats, and to add to the frustration, those who used to offer to help her out of the kindness of their hearts now expected to be paid. And she was left with the best friends money can buy.

I lost my husband, my house, my business, and my finances and couldn't afford the best of anything. But God sent me the very best. They called themselves *friends,* but I have always known they were angels who helped me find a rental house and became movers, painters, financial planners, cleaners, handymen, plumbers, electricians, counselors, and encouragers. They endured my endless indecision, and through it all, they loved me without condition or pay. I treasure each one.

I raise my coffee cup to the ones who won the lottery. But their winnings cannot top mine.

> Friends love through all kinds of weather, and families stick together in all kinds of trouble. (Proverbs 17:17 MSG)

"Thanks" seems so inadequate.

The Forecast

The weather reporter said, "Black ice and snow," and clarified, "A storm is coming in from the northwest, bringing rain, wind, and freezing temperatures." We went out and bought scads of stuff we needed and scads of stuff we didn't, because we were going be stuck in our homes for a week. But we weren't. The forecast was off.

Two weeks later ... They said "snow and sleet," and clarified, "A storm is sweeping in from the southwest with freezing temperatures." We had heard it all before and went to work anyway. In a matter of a few hours, highways became icy nightmares of jack-knifed trailers and stranded motorists. We had ignored the wrong forecast.

Jesus forecasted "born again" and clarified, "I am the Way, the Truth and the Life. Nobody comes to the Father except by me." He provided the sacrifice. Some listened and others ignored Him, even though *He has never forecasted wrong. Ever.* Networks give out their forecasts based upon guesswork; He gives out His forecast based upon truth. Make sure you know the difference.

> When you pass through the waters, I will be with you; when you pass through the rivers, they will not sweep over you. When you walk through the fire, you will not be burned; the flames will not set you ablaze. (Isaiah 43:2 NIV)

Now, that's a forecast you can trust.

Broken Stuff

Friends tell you to *let it go*, but you can't quit thinking about the way it was when things were perfect. It's time to come face-to-face with reality: *Things were never perfect.* Even if you had been given everything you needed to make things perfect, you still couldn't. But God can use broken stuff.

Gideon gathered thirty-two thousand guys together to fight the enemy, and odds were still four-to-one favoring the bad guys. God told Gideon He didn't need this gigantic army to win. "I can win this thing with three hundred men, three hundred clay pots and three hundred torches. If you play it My way, you've already won" (from Judges 6).

God uses broken stuff. He took Gideon's army, broke it up, and used the pieces of fire and pottery to bring glory to His name. This was not the way Gideon imagined it would go down.

You may be living a life you didn't imagine would go down the way it has. But God, who continues to work things together for your good, is in restoration mode. *You can fight the war your way, or you can win the war His way.* The Healer, Provider, Protector, and Deliverer works in sickness, loss, and discouragement. And He specializes in *broken stuff.*

Need further proof? Google: *donkey jawbone.*

The End

"The guy was really dead all along," they told me and ruined the movie. You may find yourself at the edge of the valley of the shadow of death, wishing you knew the ending to your story.

You cannot press *fast-forward* or *rewind*, and nobody can accurately give you any more information about the end of your story than you already have. Remote-control living is an impossibility. God is interested in your whole story. Your conception began long before you drew your first breath, and you will be with Him long after you take your last breath on earth. But you are invited to be a witness to His great work in your life in the middle, where you are right now.

Life takes us all through some intense situations, back down to living in the land of the dull. But when you trust Christ, you understand His words: "This, too shall pass." Every experience is temporary, but within these temporary places, you will witness God's nourishment and protection.

Share your story with others. Jesus saves. You will never ruin the end of anyone's movie, because it is a great comfort to be able to say, no matter what:

> The Lord is my rock, my fortress and my Savior. (2 Samuel 2:22)

He is the beginning ...

And the end.

The Beginning

For God so loved the world, He gave His only
begotten Son, that whosoever believes in Him, will
not perish, but have everlasting life. (John 3:16)

Moose Manor

I found the cottage I call Moose Manor during one of the darkest times of my life. In every lonely hour, I have praised the *God of the gift of the cottage.* I rent to buy.

Inside her walls and on her porches, I find the gift of His presence, His words, His direction and redirection. When He's quiet, I have learned to value the quality of His gift: *patiently abiding.* The apostle Paul's words "When I am weak, then I am strong" finally make sense.

At six o'clock in the morning I join Him in the kitchen, and on purpose, I hear Him speak straight from His Word. The conversation is easy, and my burden becomes lighter.

I was certain I belonged here at this little cottage; but at the end of the year, when it came time for me to cough up the money to buy Moose Manor, I had nothing left. I had prayed for God to let me stay. I didn't know how He was going do it, but all along I felt He would.

One week before quittin' time, I gave Him back Moose Manor. I was ready to move on, wherever He would lead me, to whatever I could afford.

And He has made me a home with a ninety-four-year-old lady who needs my help. She calls me a blessing. I call her Mom.

Forgiveness

> So, chosen by God for this new life of love, dress in
> the wardrobe God picked out for you: compassion,
> kindness, humility, quiet strength, discipline. Be
> even-tempered, content with second place, quick to
> forgive an offense. Forgive as quickly and completely
> as the Master forgave you. And regardless of what
> else you put on, wear love. It's your basic, all-
> purpose garment. Never be without it. (Colossians
> 3:12–14 MSG)

Does forgiving mean forgetting? When my son Christian was little, he
would run across the back deck, sliding his hand across the wooden
rail. He learned rather quickly that wasn't a good thing. At the wise
old age of five, Christian counseled his little brother: "Cody, don't
put your hands near that rail. Splinters live in there."

God has given us the ability to reason: fire burns, ice freezes, and
germs spread. Because you are sensitive to the hurt you experienced,
your memory may slip back from time to time. But do not stir that
pot of anger. Remember: you have hurt God, but He forgives you
completely.

Bitterness eats you up. By forgiving others, you free yourself from its
destruction. The Enemy has held you in that cell for way too long.
You are free of the burden. Forgiveness has torn the curtain. And
now you can see Christ at work in every detail of your life.

Sometimes He puts it back together the funniest way.

Printed in the United States
By Bookmasters